CoS

AMERICAN ASTRONAUTS AND SPACECRAFT

An American astronaut named Neil Armstrong puts his left foot on the windless surface of the moon. "That's one small step for a man, one giant leap for mankind," he radioed. The time was 10:56 PM. The date was July 20, 1969.

AMERICAN ASTRONAUTS AND SPACECRAFT

A Pictorial History from Project Mercury through Project Apollo

EDITED BY DAVID C. KNIGHT

FOREWORD BY THOMAS O. PAINE
Administrator, National Aeronautics and Space Administration

"I believe we should go to the moon... before this decade is out."
President John F. Kennedy, May 25, 1961

FRANKLIN WATTS

FOR A HANDFUL OF BRAVE MEN —
AMERICAN ASTRONAUTS OF THE PAST, PRESENT,
AND FUTURE

Grateful acknowledgment is made to the National Aeronautics and Space Administration (NASA) whose Staff and Personnel cheerfully and efficiently supplied photographic and research materials for this book. In particular, I would like to thank those patient and hardworking individuals in the Public Affairs and Audio-Visual sections of NASA who provided not only editorial materials but good advice and encouraging words during the assembling of this volume. Any inadvertancies or errors in captional text, commentary, or chronology remain mine alone, and do not alter or reflect official NASA information. Readers must, however, allow for variations in future biographical data as they develop, which may render incomplete in the present printing those short biographical sketches of American astronauts presented at the end of this work. — DCK

FOREWORD

"In the course of human history, no decade has presented more of a challenge to the mind and creative ingenuity of man than has the past ten-year period of space exploration. For in those brief years, the United States Manned Space Program has turned an age-old dream of mystics and visionaries into an accomplished reality.

"We have sent men to the moon. We have unmanned spacecraft far beyond it. But these accomplishments, impressive as they are, are only the beginning. As we read the pictorial history unfolded in this volume, it is evident that we have started out on the most impressive epoch of scientific development the world has ever known.

"Because of the Space Program, young people today can look forward to altogether fresh opportunities far beyond any ever given a previous generation: opportunities that will test their minds, their skills, and their courage, broadening their vision of man's role in the universe. They will learn new sciences of space, have a new cosmology to frame their concepts, and gain a new view and understanding of not just our own planet but our solar system as well.

"For it is clear that man's future destiny lies in space. This nation in which we live—and all others on the face of the earth—will never be the same again."

Thomas O. Paine
Administrator
National Aeronautics and
Space Administration

CONTENTS

1   Project Mercury / 8

2   Project Gemini / 34

3   Project Apollo / 84

Brief Biographies of United States Astronauts / 133

A Glossary of Space Terms / 147

Index / 156

Color plates follow page 64

1. PROJECT MERCURY

Organized in October, 1959, Project Mercury's objectives were to orbit a manned spacecraft about the earth, investigate man's reaction to — and his abilities in — space flight, and recover safely both man and spacecraft.

Astronauts Alan B. Shepard and Virgil I. Grissom made sub-orbital flights on May 5 and July 21, 1961, respectively. Both men flew as high as 115 miles above the earth and landed in the Atlantic Ocean about 300 miles from their launch site at Cape Kennedy (then Cape Canaveral), Florida. These two fledgling flights lasted but a bare quarter of an hour each.

The following year, on February 20, 1962, John H. Glenn, Jr., flew three times around the world in his spacecraft, Friendship 7. He thus became the first American to orbit his home planet, the earth. Glenn was followed three months later by M. Scott Carpenter, who also orbited the earth three times in Aurora 7. Flight time for both astronauts was nearly the same — 4 hours and 50-odd minutes. Carpenter spent much of his mission initiating research experiments to further future space efforts. A few months later, Walter M. Schirra, Jr., in Sigma 7 made a six-orbit flight, during which he developed techniques and procedures applicable to extended time in space. And on May 16, 1963, L. Gordon Cooper, Jr., in Faith 7 splashed down successfully after a 22-orbit flight to complete the Mercury Program. Cooper met the final objective of the program by spending a day in space.

The Project Mercury flights answered many questions for future explorers of space. They proved that man could withstand the powerful gravity forces of takeoff and reentry into the terrestrial atmosphere, and that he could withstand weightlessness during space flight. In addition, Mercury astronauts discovered that they were able to make observations in space flight, perform routine tasks, and conduct experiments almost as easily as they could in conventional aircraft.

"We Seven" the first American astronaut team called themselves. Selected in April of 1959, barely six months after the National Aeronautics and Space Administration was established, the seven original astronauts were: (front row, from left) Walter M. Schirra, Jr., Donald K. ("Deke") Slayton, John H. Glenn, Jr., M. Scott Carpenter; (back row, from left) Alan B. Shepard, Jr., Virgil I. ("Gus") Grissom, and L. Gordon Cooper.

Training and equipment were the best the United States could provide. Shown here on the launching pad is a Mercury-Redstone booster rocket used in the two Mercury suborbital flights. Pencil-like "cherry picker" at right has been positioned for removal of astronaut in a last-minute emergency during countdown. In background is the gantry used for preparing the spacecraft and rocket; it is removed to the edge of the pad about an hour before lift-off. Here, Mercury capsule has been mated to the booster.

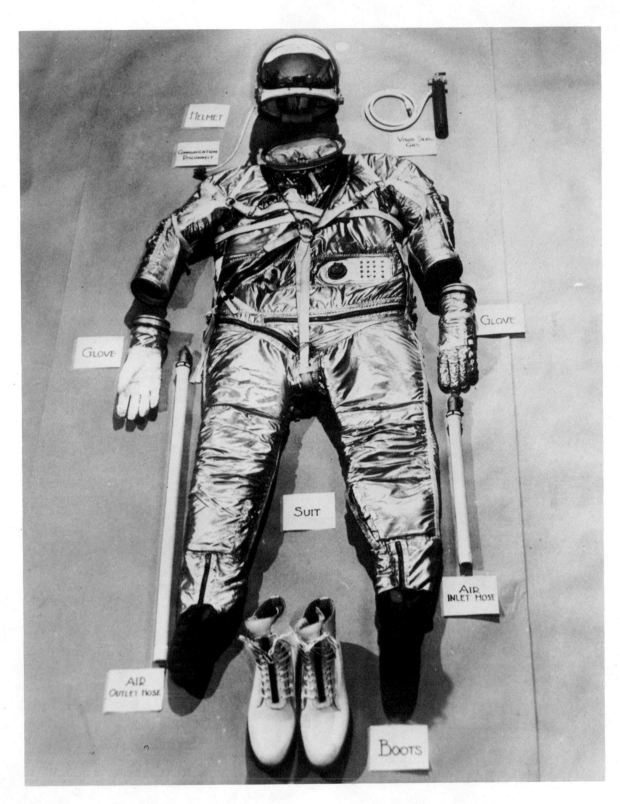

What the well-dressed Mercury astronaut wore — with associated equipment and gear — labeled and laid out for inspection. Suits were later refined and improved to meet new contingencies.

At left: America's first three Project Mercury astronauts in space were (from left) John Glenn, Virgil Grissom, and Alan Shepard. Shown here suited up and still in training before the first suborbital launch, they grin confidently as posed before the Mercury-Redstone booster rocket and spacecraft capsule on the launch pad at Cape Canaveral, Florida.

At right: The complicated process of suiting up is demonstrated here by astronaut Gordon Cooper. It was just one of the many simulated tests undergone in preparing for the first manned space flights.

Below: Mercury astronauts (from left) Glenn, Shepard, and Grissom trade wisecracks in Hangar S during preflight preparations for the manned suborbital flights.

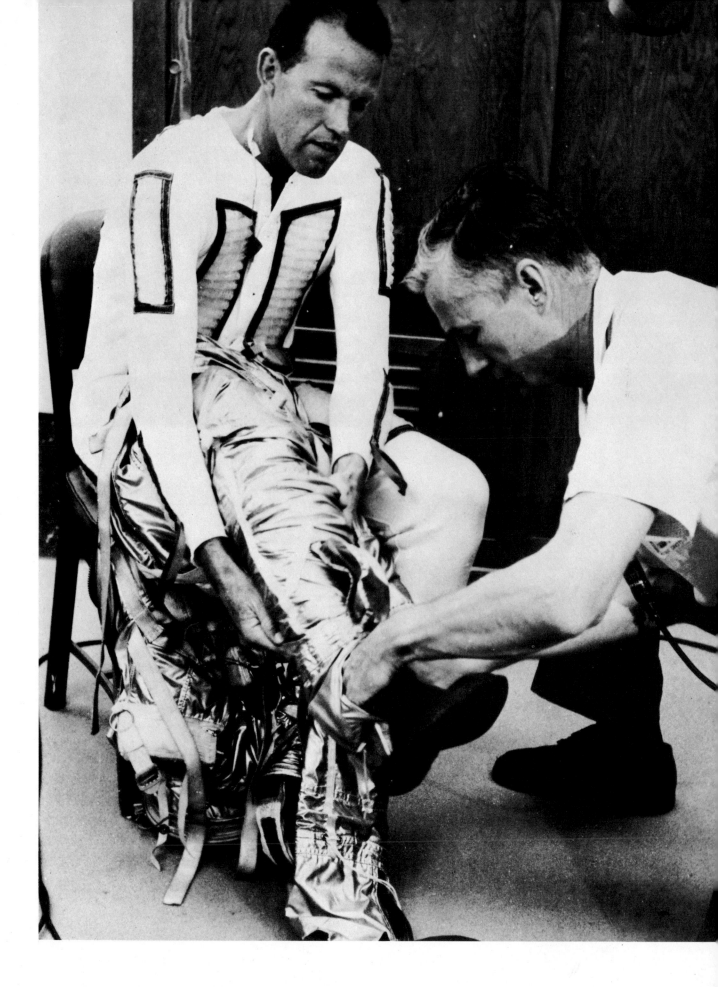

Rigorous testing was undergone by Mercury astronauts before the suborbital flights. Above, John Glenn is being subjected to centrifuge testing at the U.S. Navy installation at Johnsville, Pennsylvania. Below, he undergoes special respiratory tests as part of the flight training program.

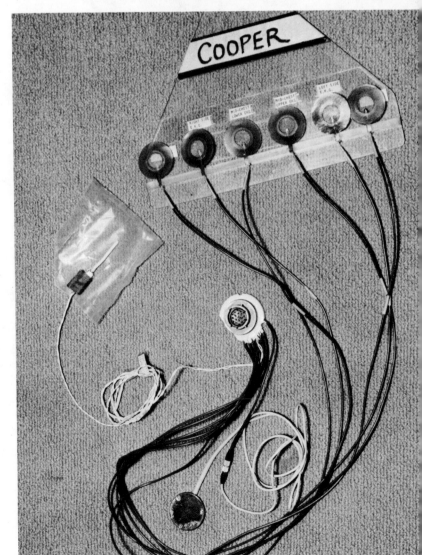

Space food. An astronaut's in-flight menu included a number of items. At top left are bite-size portions of ready-to-eat food. Plastic bags contain newer dehydrated varieties which are combined with water and mixed in the bags before consumption. Pictured here are shrimp, potato salad, and apple juice.

Each astronaut had his individual set of bio-sensors which were attached to his body during space flight in order to monitor heart and respiration rates. Astronauts also took their own temperatures with oral thermometers (top center); these also doubled as checks on suit temperature when not in use.

One of the most vital phases of training was egress from the space capsule after simulated splashdown. Here astronaut Virgil Grissom squeezes out of the narrow neck of the capsule and rips open his survival kit which contains inflatable one-man life raft, portable emergency radio transmitter, and other gear.

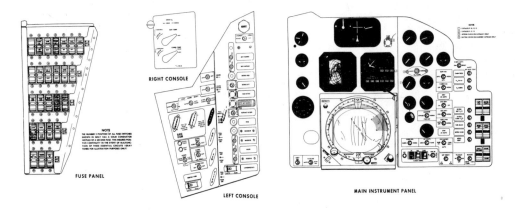

FUSE PANEL

RIGHT CONSOLE

LEFT CONSOLE

MAIN INSTRUMENT PANEL

Part of the astronauts' training was knowing their instrument panels and consoles inside out.

The big day comes. On the morning of May 5, 1961, all seven Project Mercury astronauts and Dr. William K. Douglas join for breakfast prior to Alan Shepard's suborbital flight. From left, facing camera, are Dr. Douglas, astronauts Glenn, Shepard, Carpenter, and Schirra. With backs to camera are Cooper, Grissom, and Slayton.

The Mercury-Redstone booster carrying America's first manned spacecraft lifts off successfully at Cape Canaveral. Alan Shepard's suborbital flight time lasted 15 minutes and 22 seconds.

Movie camera inside Freedom 7 spacecraft took this picture of Shepard as he was about to raise the shield in front of his face during descent after the opening of the main parachute.

Marine helicopter lifts Freedom 7 from the Atlantic Ocean after splashdown. Shepard is already aboard the chopper and will be airlifted back to the carrier U.S.S. *Champlain* for medical debriefing and a physical.

Astronaut Shepard inspects his spacecraft following his return to the carrier.

Second man in space for America was astronaut Virgil I. ("Gus") Grissom, shown here preparing to enter Liberty Bell 7. Grissom's successful suborbital flight took him to an altitude of 118 statute miles at a speed of 5,310 mph. After a flight of nearly 16 minutes, he landed about 305 miles down range from Cape Canaveral and 145 miles northeast of Grand Bahama Island.

Left, Grissom lifts off. After splashdown there was trouble. The explosive mechanism on Gus's escape hatch was accidentally activated. The hatch tore open, and the astronaut had to swim to safety as the space capsule sank beneath him. Helicopter (right) has hooked on to Liberty Bell 7, but minutes later had to release it since it was full of seawater. A few years later, on January 27, 1967, Gus Grissom's luck ran out: He was one of the three astronauts killed in a flash fire during a preflight practice session of Apollo I.

America's first manned orbital space flight was made by astronaut John H. Glenn on February 20, 1962. Here he poses for the camera beside his famous spacecraft, Friendship 7, about a month before he went up. Below, Glenn kept in trim for the flight by taking morning runs on Cocoa Beach, Florida.

Ignition and lift-off! Glenn is on his way. This view of NASA Manned Spacecraft Center's Mercury-Atlas 6 records a historic moment as the mighty booster rocket propels the astronaut's space capsule on its three orbits of the world. Glenn's official flight time was 4 hours, 55 minutes, and 23 seconds. That day the astronaut enjoyed *four* sunsets.

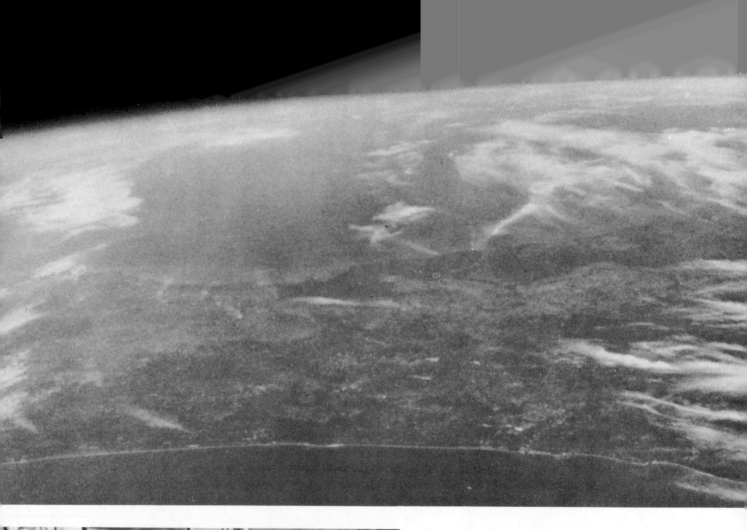

"Oh, the view is tremendous!" exclaimed Glenn in rapt admiration of his home planet from his vantage point in space. Above is what the astronaut saw at the beginning of his second orbit. Through the window of Friendship 7, Glenn shot this picture of the Florida coast. It was taken at about a 100-mile altitude while Glenn's spacecraft was traveling at 17,500 mph.

Naval personnel of the destroyer *Noa* hook on recovery equipment to Friendship 7 after splashdown. But Glenn had run into serious trouble with the small rockets that controlled the craft's altitude. Forced to take over control manually, Glenn did so safely and successfully. Next, the Mercury capsule's heat shield, needed for a safe reentry, had become unlatched. The astronaut was lucky — the heat shield held and he landed safely.

Top: With relief apparent on his face after the ordeal of the heat shield, Glenn relaxes in the wardroom of the carrier U.S.S. *Randolph.* Below: President John F. Kennedy pins the NASA Distinguished Service Award Medal on astronaut Glenn. Later, Glenn addressed a joint session of Congress and received a standing ovation.

Second American to orbit the earth was M. Scott Carpenter. In his Mercury capsule Aurora 7, the astronaut completed three orbits on May 24, 1962. His flight time was nearly identical with Glenn's—4 hours and 56 minutes. Here, about a month before the mission, Carpenter relaxes for a moment before starting a run in the procedures trainer.

Carpenter, too, ran into a bit of trouble. His space capsule overshot the splash-down point by some 250 miles, putting the astronaut temporarily out of contact with his rescuers. After spending three hours in his life raft, he was picked up in the Atlantic Ocean and airlifted by helicopter to the carrier U.S.S. *Intrepid.* Right, a happy Scott Carpenter strolls across the carrier's flight deck after his pickup.

Astronaut Walter M. Schirra, Jr., was the third American to orbit the earth, on October 3, 1962. In his spacecraft Sigma 7, he achieved the first scheduled landing in the Pacific Ocean. Schirra is shown here completely suited up. Connected to the pressurized suit is his portable air-conditioning unit. Miniature Mercury spacecraft with escape tower is on his left.

The Atlas launch vehicle lifts off success-fully, carrying Schirra in Sigma 7. He completed six orbits in 9 hours and 13 minutes. Below, a Navy frogman scrambles astride the flotation collar, as a line secured to the top of Sigma 7 pulls it toward the prime recovery ship *Kearsarge.*

Astronaut L. Gordon ("Gordo") Cooper was the first American to spend a full day in space. In fact, he spent almost a day and a half in orbital flight — officially recorded as 34 hours, 19 minutes, and 49 seconds. During May 15 to 16, 1963, Cooper in his spacecraft Faith 7 made 22 complete revolutions of the earth. In so doing, "Gordo" met the final objective of the Mercury program — an astronaut's capability of living and working in space for at least twenty-four hours.

Cooper snapped many pictures from Faith 7. On his eighth orbit at an altitude of
100 miles, he took one of cloud formations over the Hankow-Yangtze area (above).
Below, Luzon in the Philippines from 117 miles above the earth.

Near the end of Cooper's 22 orbits around the earth, a malfunction occurred in the auto pilot, forcing the astronaut to take the controls manually. He guided himself down perfectly — within four miles from the carrier *Kearsarge* and in sight of those aboard it. As Cooper put it, he landed "right on the old gazoo." Minutes later, frogmen (above) were attaching the flotation collar to Faith 7. Left, a happy Gordo Cooper talks to his wife in Houston, Texas, from the *Kearsarge*.

A reception at the White House signals the end of Project Mercury. President John F. Kennedy congratulates Gordon Cooper after his successful 22-orbit mission. Cooper's fellow astronauts — Grissom, Shepard, Schirra, and Carpenter — Vice-President Johnson, and other dignitaries look on.

2. PROJECT GEMINI

Using the knowledge and know-how gained in Project Mercury, American astronauts launched Project Gemini. The operation took its name from the Greek word meaning "twin," since each flight would carry a complement of two astronauts. Gemini's goals were fourfold: to carry out experiments requiring participation and supervision of men aboard the spacecraft; to develop rendezvous and docking techniques; to find out how men would perform and behave during an orbital flight lasting several days; and to demonstrate controlled reentry into the earth's atmosphere and splashing down at a predetermined site.

Designated Gemini 3, the first manned Gemini flight took place on March 23, 1965. Virgil I. Grissom and John W. Young, popularly dubbed the "Gemini twins," orbited planet earth three times in 4 hours and nearly 53 minutes. It was America's first two-man space flight and the "twins" were the first pilots to steer their craft in flight. During that mission they altered their orbital path by firing tiny retro-rockets that were computer-controlled. As for Gus Grissom, he became America's first astronaut to make a second space trip.

The second manned flight, Gemini 4, blasted off on June 3, 1965, with astronauts James A. McDivitt, command pilot, and Edward H. White aboard. After orbiting the earth 62 times in 97 hours and 56 minutes of flight, they splashed down in the Atlantic Ocean. On the third revolution, Ed White emerged from the spacecraft for his famous "space walk," while McDivitt remained at the controls. Remaining outside for 21 minutes, White shot a number of pictures, including the first photo ever taken of a spacecraft in space from a vantage point outside the craft. This flight also chalked up the first extensive maneuver of a spacecraft by the pilot.

During the eight-day flight of Gemini 5, from August 21 to 29, 1965, astronauts L. Gordon Cooper and Charles Conrad, Jr., broke a number of existing manned space-flight records. They completed 120 orbits about the earth — over 3.3 million miles —

in 190 hours and 55 minutes. Their 8-day flight demonstrated man's capacity for sustained functioning in space environment.

The world's longest manned orbital flight to date — a whopping 206 revolutions of the earth in 330 hours and 35 minutes — was performed by Gemini 7 between December 4 and 18, 1965. Aboard were astronauts Frank Borman and James A. Lovell, Jr. They photographed the moon and performed many experiments, including shedding their space suits in flight and flying in formation with the detached second phase of the booster rocket.

On December 15, eleven days after Gemini 7 began its 14-day flight, Gemini 6, piloted by astronauts Walter Schirra and Thomas P. Stafford, blasted off. The huge booster rocket lifted them into an elliptical orbit that caused their craft to approximate the path of their sister ship, Gemini 7. Then, due to skillful maneuvering of their craft, the astronauts were able slowly to close the distance between themselves and Gemini 7. In fact, the two spacecraft at one point were only inches apart. Thus, for the first time in history, two spacecraft, with men aboard each, flew in formation. It was the world's initial successful space rendezvous. Both astronaut crews accomplished their missions with flawless precision. And, in addition to conducting many valuable medical experiments, the Gemini 7 crew managed to make other scientific contributions. They were able to sight stars and take "fixes" by a hand-held sextant, thus determining their position in space and proving that men in space are capable of navigating without the aid of computers. Moreover, the astronauts registered infrared readings of ionized air molecules formed when their craft reentered the atmosphere of the earth, and they communicated with earth by laser-beam transmission methods.

On March 16, 1966, astronauts Neil A. Armstrong and David Scott in Gemini 8 lifted off successfully. After four revolutions of the earth, the spacecraft rendezvoused and docked with an Agena target vehicle. It was the first successful docking maneuver of two orbiting spacecraft. However, the crew of Gemini 8 was not able to carry out its entire mission and had to abort, due to spinning of the spacecraft and the Agena vehicle. The astronauts were forced to make an emergency landing in the Pacific Ocean after concluding 6.5 orbits of the earth.

Lifted into orbit on June 3, 1966, was Gemini 9, piloted by astronauts Thomas P. Stafford and Eugene A. Cernan. The flight, which lasted 72 hours and 20 minutes, achieved 45 revolutions of the earth, during which Gemini 9 rendezvoused three times with the Agena target vehicle. There was also an extravehicular exercise — a two hour and seven minute space walk by astronaut Cernan.

The following month — on July 18 to 21, 1966 — saw the 43-orbit flight of Gemini 10, with pilots John W. Young and Michael Collins aboard. These astronauts wrote a brand new chapter in the space handbook. Gemini 10 rendezvoused and docked with the Agena target vehicle and then fired Agena's rocket engines to propel itself to a new altitude record — 475 miles above the earth. It was the first use of a target vehicle as a source of propellant power after docking. In addition, Collins, in a 28-minute space walk, maneuvered in space with a hand-held jet gun.

Gemini 11 was sent aloft on September 12, 1966. During its 44-orbit, 71-hour flight, it racked up a new series of firsts. Astronauts Charles Conrad, Jr., and Richard F. Gordon, Jr., completed the first rendezvous and docking on the initial orbit. The flight also saw the first multiple docking in space, and the first formation flight of two space vehicles joined by a tether. Gemini 11 also achieved a new altitude record — about 853 miles. Astronaut Gordon also took a 40-minute space walk.

The 59-orbit, 94½-hour flight of Gemini 12 completed the highly successful Gemini space program. With astronauts James A. Lovell, Jr., and Edwin E. Aldrin, Jr., as pilots, Gemini 12 was launched November 11, 1966, and splashed down on the fifteenth. Aldrin's extravehicular activity (EVA) lasted for a record 5½ hours. Walking and working outside the orbiting spacecraft, he proved that a properly equipped and prepared astronaut can function effectively outside his space vehicle. The two men also made the first photograph of a solar eclipse from space.

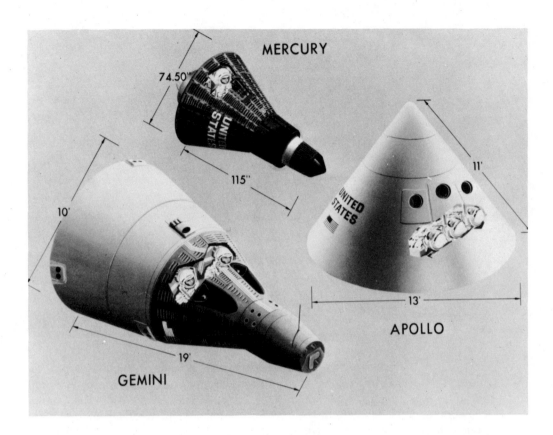

MERCURY

74.50"

UNITED STATES

115"

11'

10'

UNITED STATES

13'

19'

APOLLO

GEMINI

These sketches show the essential differences — and evolution — of the space vehicles of the three space programs. Mercury was designed for a single astronaut; Gemini for two; and Apollo for three. Cutaway view (below) of Gemini spacecraft reveals much of the basic hardware and equipment of the vehicle.

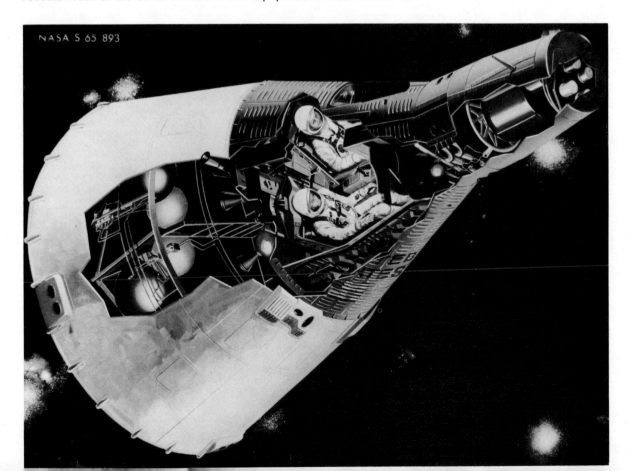

NASA S 65 893

Just as in Project Mercury, there were long days of training for the astronauts. Above, Gus Grissom and John Young undergo water egress training at Ellington Air Force Base, Texas. Below, John Young checks out a mock-up of the Gemini spacecraft at McDonnell Aircraft Corp. Young and the other astronauts have already found out how more much advanced, sophisticated, complex, and versatile the Gemini spacecraft controls are over those of the pioneering Mercury's. New subsystems have been introduced: fuel cells to replace batteries; ejection seats; onboard propulsion for maneuvering in space; and a rendezvous radar and inertial guidance system for docking missions.

Complex 19, Cape Kennedy, Florida. Here NASA's Gemini 3 spacecraft is being erected. The vehicle is being hoisted to the White Room above the massive Titan launch booster prior to the mating of the two elements.

PROJECT GEMINI | 39

Astronauts Gus Grissom and John W. Young pose in their space suits after being selected as the prime astronauts for the first manned Gemini 3 flight.

Young (foreground) and Grissom walk up the ramp to the elevator that will take them to the White Room atop the Gemini-Titan launch vehicle. Each carries his air-conditioning unit with him.

Historic moment on Pad 19. Lift-off of the United States, first two-man spacecraft at 9:24 A.M., March 23, 1965. The launch of Gemini 3 was a near perfect one, under clear skies. The vehicle carrying Grissom and Young was injected into a 100- to 139-mile-orbit of the earth.

The Gemini 3 "space twins" splashed down some 60 miles short of the carrier U.S.S. *Intrepid* near Grand Turk Island in the West Indies. Here the spacecraft is being hoisted aboard by naval personnel. Below, Young and Grissom leave the White House, where President Johnson presented them with the NASA Exceptional Service Medal.

Prime astronauts for famed "first-walk-in-space" flight in Gemini 4 were Edward H. White, II, pilot, and James A. McDivitt, command pilot. The 62-orbit flight lasted just over four days.

Lift-off from Launch Complex 19 at Cape Kennedy was at 10:16 A.M., June 3, 1965. The Gemini 4 spacecraft was injected into a 100- to 175-mile-orbit of the earth.

Shown here is a model of the extravehicular suit worn by Ed White for his "space walk." Suit differed from the regular Gemini suit in three ways: An extra layer was added for thermal and micrometeoroid protection; two external visors were attached to the helmet; and a strain-relief zipper was added. The basic Gemini suit was a close-fitting full-pressure suit with an inner layer of rubberized material covered by nylon. Helmet and gloves could be removed in flight.

Walk in space. Two views of Ed White performing his spectacular extravehicular (EVA) feat during the third orbit of the Gemini 4 flight. He is secured to the spacecraft by a 25-foot umbilical line and a 23-foot tether, both wrapped together with gold tape to form one cord. White wears an emergency oxygen supply chest pack and is holding a hand-held self-maneuvering unit which he used to move about in his weightless environment. He remained outside the craft for 21 minutes. But, as would be the case with his fellow astronaut Gus Grissom, White's luck would give out some two years hence. He was destined to be one of the astronauts killed when fire destroyed the cabin of Apollo 1 early in 1967.

This spectacular photo of earth terrain taken by the Gemini flight crew shows the Hadramaut Plateau in the southern part of the Arabian Peninsula, with the Gulf of Aden and Somalia in the background.

View (above) of the *limb* — earth's outer edge of brightness — was taken aboard Gemini 4 as the spacecraft approached the daylight side of the earth. Below, astronauts White and McDivitt are greeted after their Atlantic splashdown and pickup aboard the carrier U.S.S. *Wasp* on June 7, 1965.

The Gemini 5 astronauts were L. Gordon ("Gordo") Cooper, Jr., and Charles Conrad, Jr., shown here suited up for a simulated test a few days before the actual flight. Their eight-day mission, from August 21 to 29, achieved the longest manned space flight to date.

As photographed from Gemini 5, this spectacular view of southern California shows the Salton Sea and Imperial Valley. From the orbiting spacecraft the view is toward the north.

Tracking stations around the world followed the progress of Gemini 5 on each revolution. This one at headquarters North American Air Defense Command (NORAD) at Colorado Springs is tracing the spacecraft on its Iconorama display at Combat Operations Center, after which it relayed the information to NASA. Canadian officer (left) also observed the display board. Below, splashdown of Gemini 5 occurred at about 8:00 A.M. on August 29, 1965. Frogmen of the U.S.S. *Lake Champlain* place the flotation collar around the space vehicle in preparation for pickup. Although the astronauts discovered that their newly designed fuel cell system began losing power early in the mission, they were able to complete the flight.

Bewhiskered astronauts Conrad (above, left) and Cooper grin happily as they come aboard the carrier *Lake Champlain*. Below, the astronauts chat via radio telephone hookup with President Johnson.

Prime astronauts selected as Gemini 7 crew were (left) James A. Lovell, Jr., pilot, and Frank Borman, command pilot. Here they pose in conventional flight suits and helmets beside an American flag a few days prior to their flight in Gemini 6. The Gemini 6/7 mission was the most complicated to date — and a demanding team effort. Scheduled to last up to 14 days, the Gemini 7 mission served as a target vehicle for the Gemini 6 spacecraft. Gemini 6 would be launched later for the rendezvous with Gemini 7.

Preparations for the 14-day Gemini 7 flight were extensive. Above are numerous items of aerospace equipment ready for stowage aboard the spacecraft. Below is the complete food supply as it appeared prior to stowage. Food packages were tied in sequence for 28 man-days — the complete supply for the two-week mission.

An overall view of the Mission Operations Control Room at Mission Control Center, Houston, Texas, moments before lift-off of Gemini 7. Flight information is displayed on TV monitors, indicator lights, and digital readout devices on the individual consoles. It is also displayed on the large group display screens at the front of the room. Below, flight controller Christopher C. Kraft, Jr., at his console in Mission Control during lift-off of the spacecraft.

Gemini 7 makes a perfect lift-off on December 4, 1965. Astronauts Borman and Lovell are on their way for the world's longest manned orbital flight — 206 orbits of the earth.

First rendezvous in space! This photo of Gemini 7 was taken through the hatch window of Gemini 6 during the station-keeping maneuvers at an altitude of 160 miles above the earth on December 15, 1965.

Left, after splashdown in the western Atlantic on December 18, Command Pilot Frank Borman is hoisted from the water by a recovery helicopter from the carrier U.S.S. *Wasp.*

Jovial and bewhiskered, astronauts Lovell and Borman arrive aboard the *Wasp*. Later (below), they examine the scorched heat shield of their Gemini 7 spacecraft. Impact marks were made on the shield during reentry into the earth's atmosphere.

Prime astronauts for the Gemini 6 rendezvous mission were Thomas P. Stafford (left), pilot, and Walter M. Schirra, command pilot. Launch was originally scheduled for December 12, 1965, but there was trouble on the launch pad. The astronauts nearly triggered their ejection mechanism when a loose electrical plug in the booster rocket caused the engines to shut down after initial firing.

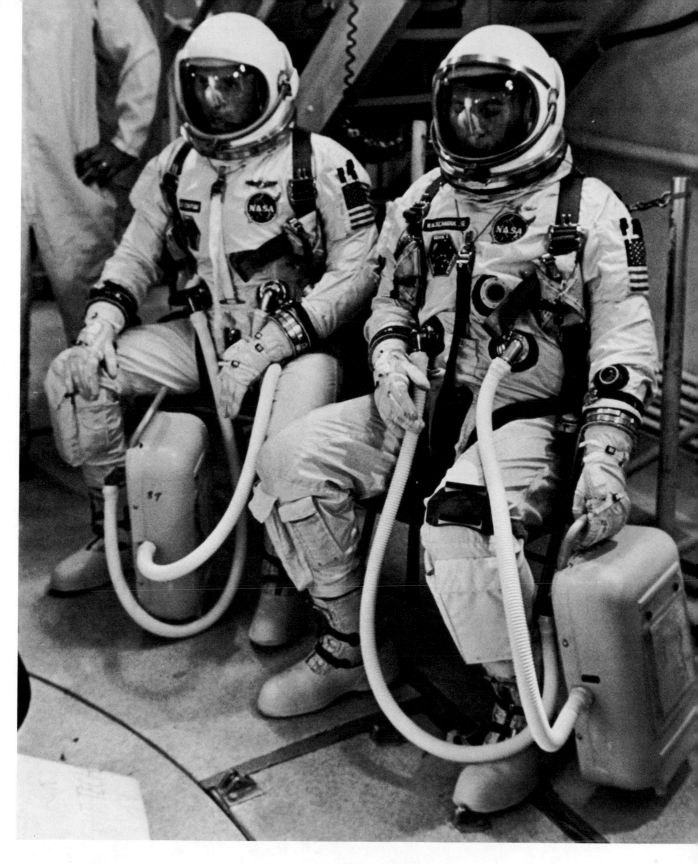

Three days later, on December 15, 1965, Gemini 6 lifted off successfully. Here astronauts Stafford and Schirra take a momentary rest in the White Room atop Pad 19 prior to boarding the spacecraft.

First space rendezvous. Gemini 6 astronauts photograph Gemini 7 spacecraft on December 15, 1965. The Gemini 7 crew, astronauts Borman and Lovell, went on to complete their two-week mission, while the Gemini 6 astronauts splashed down in the western Atlantic area on December 16. Below, Wally Schirra stands up in the spacecraft to stretch while awaiting the arrival of the recovery carrier *Wasp*. A three-man Navy frogman team is assisting in the operation.

Above, Schirra and Stafford triumphantly shake each other's hand as they arrive aboard the carrier after their highly successful rendezvous mission with Gemini 7. Not only was Gemini 6 able to catch Gemini 7, but the two spacecraft flew together in tight formation for some distance. Below, sailors gather to watch the astronauts slice into cake that was part of their warm welcome after pickup by the *Wasp*.

Prime crew for the Gemini 8 mission were astronauts David R. Scott (left) and Neil A. Armstrong. Both men were making their first space flight. Here they wait in the White Room at Cape Kennedy for the order to board the spacecraft. The mission was scheduled to last for three days and its objectives included rendezvous and docking attempts with an orbiting Agena target vehicle, and a nearly three-hour space walk by astronaut Scott.

64 | PROJECT GEMINI

Astronaut John Glenn and his spacecraft Friendship 7 during Project Mercury.

Gemini 4 astronaut Ed White performing his famous "walk in space."

A Project Gemini launch vehicle lifts off from Cape Kennedy, Florida.

A view of the Gemini 6 spacecraft carrying astronauts Schirra and Stafford, with earth horizon at right.

Superb color photography shows astronaut James Lovell being hoisted to the recovery helicopter from the Gemini 7 spacecraft below, after splashdown.

A remarkable photo of Gemini 7 as photographed from the Gemini 6 spacecraft during the world's first successful space rendezvous.

Lower California as seen from Gemini 9. Below, astronauts Conrad and Gordon photographed this view of the earth looking northward from Iran and Saudi Arabia, with India on the horizon.

Sinai peninsula, Nile Valley, and the Red Sea as photographed from Gemini 12.

A view of the target adapter during docking maneuvers, as seen from Gemini 9.

Apollo 7's discarded upper Saturn 4 stage, with a portion of the Gulf of Mexico below.

A view of the earth from Apollo 8, showing nearly the whole of the Western Hemisphere. Below, the earth viewed by the Apollo 8 astronauts as they orbited the moon.

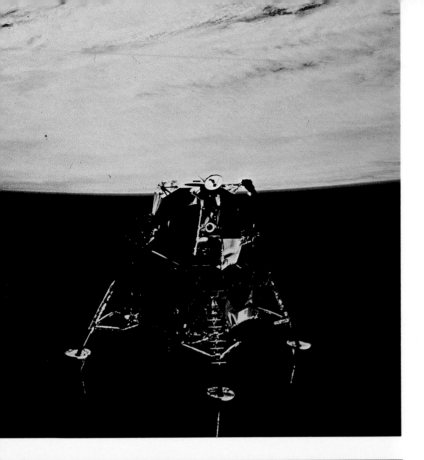

The Apollo 9 lunar module as seen from the command/service module.

An excellent view of the docked Apollo 9 command/service module and lunar module "Spider," with the earth below.

As photographed from the Apollo 9 command module "Gumdrop," a view of the lunar module still attached to the Saturn 5 third stage.

Astronauts McDivitt and Schweickart took this spectacular picture of the command/service module, showing the earth below, from the lunar module.

Earth-rise as seen from Apollo 10, with the lunar Seas of Serenity (light hues), Tranquility, and Fertility below.

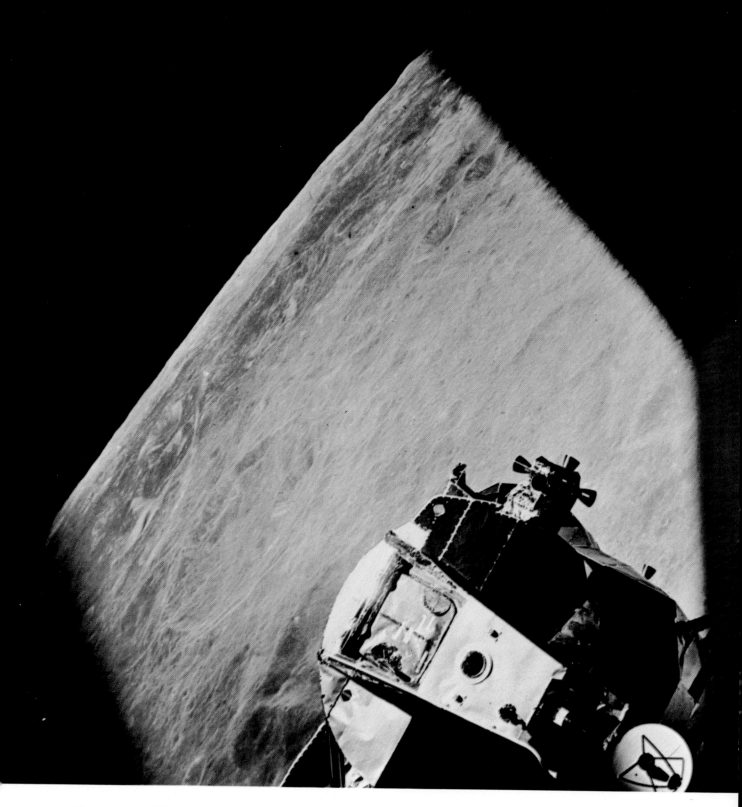

The far side of the moon as seen by Apollo 10 astronauts, with the lunar module approaching the command module.

Astronaut Aldrin walks on the surface of the moon near the leg of the lunar module during Apollo 11 extravehicular activity.

In this famous photo, astronaut Armstrong (who was taking the picture) and the lunar module are reflected in Aldrin's face mask.

Earth rises above the lunar horizon as the Apollo 11 ascent stage nears the command and service module for the docking rendezvous.

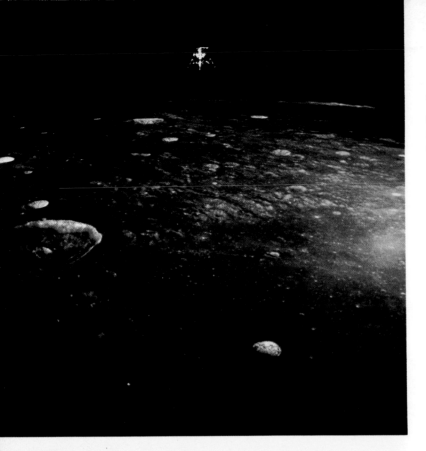

The Apollo 12 lunar module Intrepid is shown here separated from the command module and heading for the landing site on the moon's Ocean of Storms.

Weird sun glare in camera's lens seems to illuminate Apollo 12 astronauts Conrad and Bean as they work on the moon's Ocean of Storms.

Right, the space suit and extravehicular equipment which was to have been worn by David Scott on his space walk. However, mission had to be terminated on the sixth orbit, due to an electrical short circuit in a yaw thruster. But the same equipment would be worn by later space walkers. Helmet is equipped with a gold-plated visor to shield the astronaut's face from unfiltered sunrays. System included a life support pack worn on the chest and a support pack worn on the back. Below, a close-up of the chest pack with its various gear.

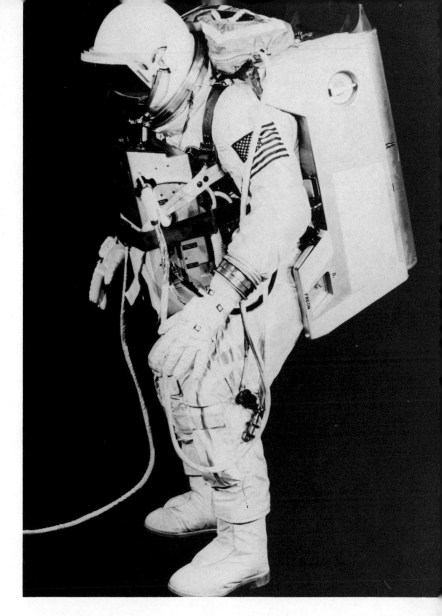

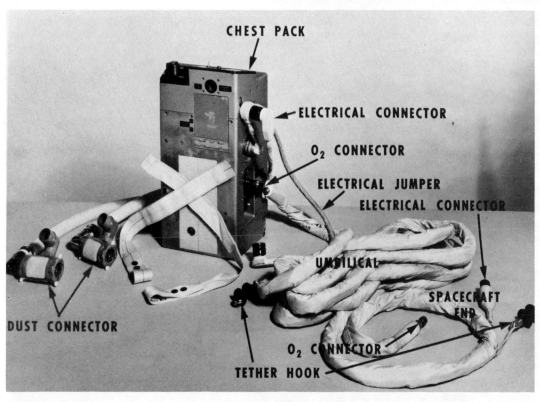

CHEST PACK

ELECTRICAL CONNECTOR

O₂ CONNECTOR

ELECTRICAL JUMPER

ELECTRICAL CONNECTOR

UMBILICAL

SPACECRAFT END

DUST CONNECTOR

O₂ CONNECTOR

TETHER HOOK

David Scott took this picture of the Agena target docking vehicle from the window of Gemini 8 during the spacecraft's approach for the rendezvous and station-keeping maneuver. The target vehicle is about 210 feet away. Below, the docked Agena vehicle with Gemini 8 — the first such docking of two vehicles in space history.

The mission terminated prematurely with splashdown in the Pacific Ocean some 500 miles east of Okinawa. Astronauts Scott and Armstrong are still seated in the spacecraft awaiting pickup by the destroyer *Mason,* as pararescue men assist with the flotation collar.

Prime astronauts for the Gemini 9 mission were astronauts Thomas P. Stafford (left), command pilot, and Eugene A. Cernan, pilot. Here they arrive at Complex 19 at Cape Kennedy for a prelaunch test. Stafford, already a veteran of the Gemini 6 flight, would be making his second trip into space. The three-day, 45-orbit flight lifted off on June 3, 1966. The astronauts could not fulfill their planned docking mission because of mechanical failure within their target's docking collar, but did rendezvous three times with the Agena target vehicle. And Gene Cernan took a two hour and seven minute space walk.

"Like an angry alligator." That was how the yawning fiber-glass cover of the docking end of the Augmented Target Docking Adapter (ATDA) looked to Tom Stafford. These are close-up views of the target adapter as seen from Gemini 9.

This is how Gemini 9 looked to the space-walking Gene Cernan. Open hatch can be seen, as can Cernan's tether line.

This historic photo of the moment of impact of Gemini 9 at splashdown by parachute in the Atlantic Ocean was made by a NASA cameraman. It was the first such photographic record made of an American spacecraft's splashdown.

Hatches open, Cernan and Stafford emerge from Gemini 9 aboard the flight deck of the U.S.S. *Wasp.* Below, the astronauts chat with President Johnson by telephone from the carrier.

Suited up and posed before a globe of the earth that they would orbit 43 times are Gemini 10 astronauts John W. Young, command pilot, and Michael Collins, pilot. Collins would be making his first flight, while Young was a veteran of the Gemini 3 mission. Primary objective of the flight was the rendezvous and docking with an Agena target vehicle.

Fan effect multiple-exposure photo shows lift-off of Gemini 10 from Cape Kennedy on July 18, 1966. Effect was achieved — through special photographic techniques — by gantry being lowered and the Titan launch vehicle blasting off simultaneously. Gemini 10 set a new altitude record of 475 miles above the earth's surface.

Here the Agena is clearly seen through the command pilot's hatch window of the Gemini 10 spacecraft moments before actual docking took place with the target vehicle launched 100 minutes before. New altitude record was achieved by firing Agena's engines to propel Gemini 10 to this new apogee.

Below, the view from space showed this storm cloud formation near the Straits of Gibraltar. Astronaut Collins "walked" in space for nearly half an hour, and maneuvered in his weightlessness environment by means of a hand-held jet gun.

A pararescueman inflates the flotation collar under Gemini 10 following the astronauts' splashdown in the Atlantic Ocean on July 21, 1966, about 460 miles east of Cape Kennedy. Landing occurred approximately 7½ miles from the recovery ship, U.S.S. *Guadalcanal*. Below, Young and Collins, relief showing on their faces and in their eyes, unwind from the grueling flight. These men, like other astronauts before and since, have seen sights that could forever alter a person's view of his tiny terrestrial spot in the cosmos.

Shown here aboard the recovery carrier *Guam* after their astonishingly successful mission in Gemini 11, astronauts Richard Gordon, Jr. (left), and Charles Conrad, Jr., circled the globe more than 71 hours for 44 orbits. It was a record-breaking flight which began September 12, 1966, when they lifted off from Cape Kennedy atop a mighty Titan launch vehicle and attained the highest altitude to date of more than 850 miles above their home planet. Conrad and Gordon rendezvoused and docked their spacecraft with an Agena target satellite during their first revolution, sooner than any other Gemini crew before them. For the first time, too, they examined the behavior of a tethered Gemini and Agena spacecraft, and astronaut Gordon took a 40-minute space walk.

Above, astronaut Dick Gordon attaches the 100-foot-long tether line to the spacecraft, linking it to the Agena target vehicle. It was the first formation flight of two space vehicles thus joined together. Picture was taken as Gemini 11 was on its sixteenth orbit, approximately 160 miles above the earth. Right, the tether line has been jettisoned and the Agena satellite is about 75 feet from the spacecraft.

The spectacular view above shows the Agena target docking vehicle some 100 feet from Gemini 11 after disconnection of the tether between the two vehicles. Below, astronaut Gordon returns to the hatch of the spacecraft after his extravehicular activity (EVA). Beneath him is the Atlantic Ocean.

More than two thousand pictures of the earth were taken from space during the entire Gemini program. One of the more dramatic shots is the one above, taken from the Gemini 11 spacecraft at an altitude of 540 miles, showing all of India and the island of Ceylon.

Anchormen in the Gemini program were the Gemini 12 astronauts James A. Lovell, Jr. (right), and Edwin E. ("Buzz") Aldrin. On their 4-day, 59-orbit flight which lifted off on November 11, 1966, the astronauts rendezvoused and docked with an Agena target vehicle, photographed the first eclipse of the sun from space, and Aldrin set an extravehicular record of 5 hours and 30 minutes.

The view from space looked like this to Lovell and Aldrin. Here their Gemini 12 spacecraft is docked to the Agena target vehicle. Handrail used by Aldrin during his EVA can be seen in the foreground. During this mission, valuable information was gained about man's ability to function for extended periods in space.

The Gemini 12 spacecraft splashed down in the Atlantic Ocean more than 600 miles southeast of Cape Kennedy on November 15, 1966.

Above, a Navy pararescueman helps astronaut Aldrin from the spacecraft. Soon the astronauts will be picked up by helicopter and flown to the prime recovery ship U.S.S. *Wasp*. Note, at the rear of the spacecraft, the scorched heat shield that protected the astronauts during reentry into the earth's atmosphere. Below, the astronauts relax in the helicopter while being flown to the *Wasp*, where they were welcomed with the "red-carpet" treatment by the carrier's officers and personnel. The date was November 15, 1966, and the highly successful Gemini program was at an end.

3. PROJECT APOLLO

Projects Mercury and Gemini were tied to the earth. But in Project Apollo, orbiting the earth would be the starting point. The astronauts assigned to the Apollo missions would break the bonds that tied them to earth and head them out into space — eventually to orbit and land on the moon.

Project Apollo's goal — a lunar landing — was designed to be accomplished in three phases: (1) earth orbital missions of up to two weeks' duration enabling the crews to gain know-how in handling the spacecraft and carrying out experiments; (2) earth orbital flights during which astronauts could learn how to rendezvous and dock with the two-man lunar excursion module (LEM); (3) landing an actual expedition to explore the lunar surface and return to earth.

This seemingly titanic task would require the development of new spacecraft and powerful new launch vehicles. America's space engineers met the challenge. A three-man crew became the unit around which two spacecraft — a command and service module, and a lunar lander — would be developed. In addition, new test stands, new buildings, new tracking systems, new ground facilities of all kinds, had to be developed for the Apollo program.

Specifically, the three-man Apollo spacecraft consisted of three sections, or modules — a command module, a service module, and a lunar excursion module (LEM). The 12-foot-high command module, comparable to the passenger area of an airliner, was so designed that three astronauts could eat, sleep, and work in it without their pressure suits. Instrument panels, controls, and other gear were designed so that the astronauts could have some maneuverability of the craft. Of the three modules, only the command module could return to earth. The service module was so constructed that it housed fuel and rockets enabling the pilots to propel their craft into and out of lunar orbit and to change their course in flight. The command module would be jettisoned before reentry into the earth's atmosphere.

More delicate than the other modules, the lunar excursion module — unable to take the decelerations and frictional heat of reentry — measures about as high as a two-story house, weighs about 16 tons, and looks like — well, like a spider. The lunar module was designed to be a complete living and working unit in itself. It would make the descent to the moon on the thrust of a rocket engine in its belly, its spindly legs supporting it on the lunar surface. When the astronauts are ready to leave the moon, in the ascent stage, the lower portion stays behind, serving as a launch pad for the LEM's lift-off.

However, such sophisticated and weighty hardware required far more thrust than the Titan booster rockets that lifted off all ten Gemini flights. Thus were developed the mighty Saturn rockets. On February 26, 1966, an unmanned Apollo test flight was successfully launched by a Saturn 1B booster. But nearly a year later, in January of 1967, tragedy struck the U.S. space program as three astronauts — Gus Grissom, Ed White, and Roger Chaffee — were burned to death as they sat locked in the cabin of the Apollo 1 spacecraft. America — indeed the world — mourned these gallant spacemen, but despite their loss the U.S. space program went forward.

Later that year, in November of 1967, the unmanned Apollo 4 was successfully inserted into orbit by a giant among giants — the huge Saturn 5 booster rocket, which stood as tall as a 36-story building. Again, on April 4, 1968, a massive Saturn 5 booster lifted off the unmanned Apollo 6 for the second successful test launch. Despite three of the Saturn 5's eleven-rocket engines refusing to fire, the remaining eight were sufficient to place Apollo 6 into earth orbit. And, Saturn 5's payload was three times heavier than all the manned spacecraft ever placed in orbit by the United States. The stage was now set for America's manned Apollo missions.

On October 11, 1968, a Saturn 1B launch vehicle lifted Apollo 7 into nearly perfect earth orbit, with astronauts Walter Schirra, Donn Eisele, and Walter Cunningham aboard. On their 10-day, 163-orbit flight, they rendezvoused and simulated docking with the spent upper stage of their Saturn booster. They also beamed back live TV pictures which were transmitted to millions of homes.

The Apollo 8 mission went down in history as one of the great events of the century. On their memorable voyage, astronauts James Lovell, William Anders, and Frank Borman journeyed beyond the gravity of earth, circled the moon, and returned with a priceless cargo of photographs, data, and scientific observations. The technical success of the mission was almost eclipsed by its emotional impact. The sight of earth-rise beyond the moon, the view of the bleak lunar craters, the look back at earth, profoundly moved the astronauts. And on Christmas Eve, Frank Borman turned to Genesis for the Word — and a hushed world listened while each astronaut read from the verses of the story of the Creation.

Apollo 9 lifted off the pad at the Kennedy Space Center on March 3, 1969, with James A. McDivitt, David R. Scott, and Russell L. Schweickart aboard. The flight was an exercise for the lunar module, missing from previous flights, to test this last major part of the Apollo system. Maneuvering, docking, and rendezvous were performed in earth orbit, instead of near the moon. Now all the elements had been tested thoroughly. Only one more flight remained before the actual moon landing.

Apollo 10, dress rehearsal for the lunar landing, duplicated every step of the upcoming Apollo 11 mission but one: the touchdown on and lift-off from the lunar surface. On May 18, 1969, Apollo 10 rose slowly off the pad and swung out on its eight-day mission. Aboard were astronauts Thomas P. Stafford, John Young, and Eugene Cernan. The mission orbited the moon, and millions saw the docking of the command module with the lunar module on the first live color TV pictures ever seen from space. Stafford and Cernan crawled into the LEM, separated from Young in the CSM, and began the letdown toward the scarred lunar surface. There were gyration problems with the LEM and, to rendezvous with Young, Cernan and Stafford had to fly the ascent stage through difficult maneuvers. But they made it back to the command module, jettisoned the ascent stage, completed their last lunar orbit, and began the long trip back to earth. Apollo 10 had blazed the trail almost to the moon.

The mission of Apollo 11 and its fantastic success must stand as one of the great achievements in human history. Astronauts Neil A. Armstrong, Michael Collins, and Edwin E. Aldrin were launched to the moon by a Saturn 5 booster on July 16, 1969. Armstrong and Aldrin were the first men to set foot on the earth's natural satellite four days later. During their EVA — watched on TV by breathless millions back on earth — they planted their country's flag on the windless lunar surface, gathered rock samples, and performed other scientific work before rejoining Collins in the command module for the long trip back home. As Armstrong himself so aptly put it, his first footprint in the lunar dust represented "one giant leap for mankind."

Apollo 12 achieved the second manned lunar landing mission in November of the same year. While astronaut Richard F. Gordon remained in the command and service modules in lunar orbit, astronauts Charles Conrad and Alan L. Bean descended in the LEM to explore the lunar surface. During their EVA, they collected core samples for scientists back on earth and performed other scientific activities near the Ocean of Storms.

The saga of Apollo 13 remains fresh in the minds of many as a miracle of rescue work by determined and ingenious men. Astronauts James A. Lovell, Fred W. Haise, Jr., and John L. Swigert, Jr., lifted off on what was to have been the third lunar landing on April 11, 1970. Yet it was soon to become apparent that the mission was ill-starred. Due to an explosion in one of the oxygen tanks in the service module, the lunar landing mission had to be cancelled, and only a jerry-rigged arrangement built by the astronauts resulted in their safe return to earth. Using the lunar module itself as a "lifeboat," the astronauts finally jettisoned their severely damaged service module prior to reentry, and — to the relief of an anxious world — splashed down safely only a scant four miles from their recovery ship, U.S.S. *Iwo Jima*.

Just as the Apollo program was proceeding well, there was a tragic setback on January 27, 1967. During a ground test that day for a manned flight, three astronauts were burned to death as they sat locked in the command module of Apollo 1. Faulty wiring in the spacecraft's electrical system set off a raging fire in the oxygen-pure atmosphere of the sealed and pressurized cabin. The three men died before a rescue team could get to them. The three were (above, from left) Virgil I. (Gus) Grissom, a veteran of the Mercury and Gemini projects; Edward H. White, II, who had performed the first "walk in space" from Gemini 4; and rookie astronaut Roger B. Chaffee. They are pictured above a few days before the tragedy. Photo opposite shows the White Room at Launch Complex 34 and the charred Apollo 1 command module.

Development of the incredibly powerful Saturn launch vehicles was responsible for the success of the Project Apollo missions. Here, the 224-foot-high Saturn 1B carrying the Apollo 7 astronauts lifts off from Cape Kennedy's Launch Complex 34, on October 11, 1968. The mighty booster rocket generated a lift-off thrust of a staggering 1.6 million pounds of thrust, capable of inserting its payload into an orbit of well over 150 statute miles above the earth.

Prime crewmen for the Apollo 7 mission were astronauts (from left) Donn F. Eisele, command module pilot and going into space for the first time; Walter Schirra, mission commander and by this time a Projects Mercury and Gemini veteran of two space flights; and Walter Cunningham, lunar module pilot. Their trip would last for nearly 11 days and they would perform 163 circuits of their home planet.

This view of the expended Saturn 1B stage was shot from the Apollo 7 spacecraft during simulated docking maneuvers at an altitude of about 125 nautical miles, at the beginning of the third orbit. Distance between the spacecraft and the spent upper stage of the huge rocket is about 100 feet. Round white disk inside the open panels is a simulated docking target similar to that used on the lunar module. Below, the Florida coastline is visible.

During Apollo 7's 45th revolution of the earth, Donn Eisele (left) and Wally Schirra hold up a humorous sign during their first TV transmission from the spacecraft. Transmission was not only received at Kennedy Space Center, but was also relayed by satellite to Europe.

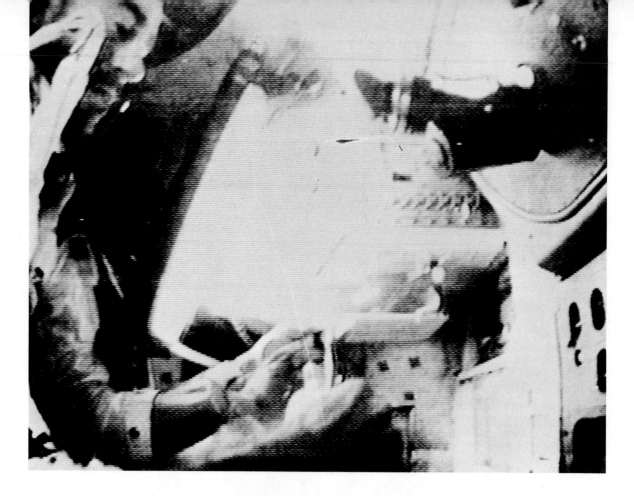

Above, astronaut Cunningham demonstrates for an earthbound TV audience how a citrus fruit drink is reconstituted in a vacuum-packaged plastic bag in the foreground. Transmission was received on the spacecraft's 76th orbit. The optical subsystems are at the astronaut's right. Right, in a TV transmission on the spacecraft's 135th revolution of the earth, Eisele scans a mission flight plan, as Walter Cunningham (left) looks on.

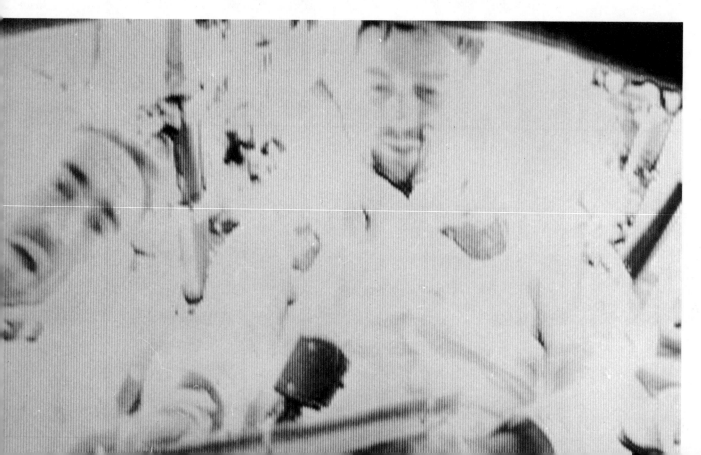

A view of the world's dozen great mountain peaks which reach a height of greater than five miles above sea level is shown in this remarkable photograph taken from Apollo 7. Mount Everest is at lower center. Other great Himalayan prominences of Nepal and Tibet are also shown.

Once a pilot, always a pilot. Here Wally Schirra checks the landing gear of the aircraft which flew him and astronauts Eisele and Cunningham from the recovery carrier *Essex* back to Cape Kennedy. The astronauts splashed down in the Atlantic Ocean on October 22, 1968, marking NASA's first successful three-man space flight.

Mightiest Saturn of them all! Generating an incredible thrust of 7.5 million pounds, this 363-foot-high Saturn 5 space vehicle carrying Apollo 8 astronauts Frank Borman, James Lovell, and William Anders lifted off on a planned lunar-orbital mission on December 21, 1968. Apollo 8 marked the first manned flight of NASA's Saturn 5 space vehicle.

Suited up for their lunar orbital mission, the Apollo 8 astronauts walk to the transfer van that took them to their Saturn 5 launch vehicle. From front to back: Frank Borman, James Lovell, and William Anders.

Astronaut Anders finds out that brushing his teeth in space is something of a problem. At the time this TV picture was transmitted, the Apollo 8 astronauts were 120,653 nautical miles into space and traveling at a velocity of 3,207 mph. Below, Mission Control at Houston, Texas, looked like this on the astronauts' third day out. On the TV monitor can be seen a picture of the earth telecast by the astronauts when they were 176,000 miles from their home planet.

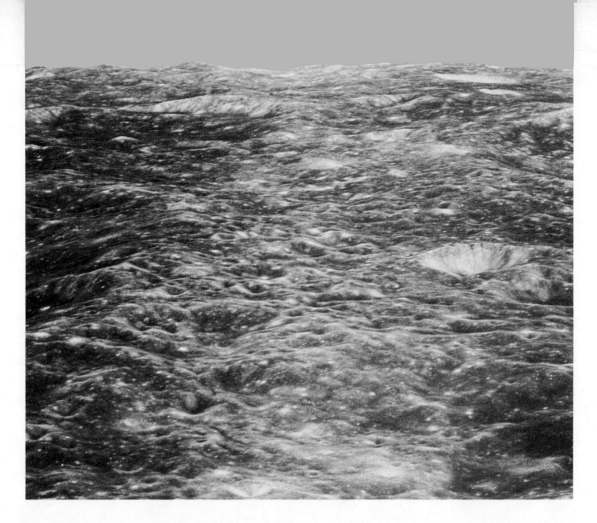

Out of touch with the earth! After their rocket engine nudged them into lunar orbit, there was a ten-minute loss of signal (LOS) during which there could be no voice contact, no tracking, no telemetering data. "We'll see you on the other side..." radioed Anders just before LOS. This photo, taken by the astronauts, was of rugged lunar terrain never before seen by man. Scene is typical of lunar far-side features illuminated by a sun that is directly overhead. Below, more far-side terrain: a crater about 110 miles in diameter with a central peak clearly visible.

This hauntingly lovely view of the rising earth greeted the astronauts as they emerged from behind the moon after the lunar orbit insertion burn. On the earth, 240,000 miles away, the sunset terminator bisects the continent of Africa. "Go ahead, Houston. Apollo 8." It was Lovell's voice coming through loud and clear, confirming their successful lunar orbital passage. The look back at their distant home profoundly moved the Apollo 8 astronauts. Said Frank Borman, "There's a beautiful earth out there. . . ."

"In the beginning there was the void ... and God created the Earth ... and it was good. ..." A scene like this inspired Frank Borman on Christmas Eve to turn to the majestic words of Genesis. Each astronaut read from the story of the Creation, and in their voices a hushed world heard what each man felt as he looked back at the tiny ball that was their home enmeshed in the black void of space. Below, Apollo 8 astronauts aboard the carrier *Yorktown* listen intently to President Johnson.

The prime crew members for the Apollo 9 mission were (from left) James A. Mc-Divitt, mission commander; David R. Scott, command module pilot; and Russell L. Schweickart, lunar module pilot. The flight lifted off the pad on March 3, 1969, with the mission of testing the last major part of the Apollo system — the lunar module. Maneuvering, rendezvous, and docking were all performed in earth orbit, instead of near the moon.

Right, the lunar module, nicknamed "Spider," is still attached to the Saturn 5 third stage. Photo was taken from the command module, called "Gumdrop." Below, three days later, an excellent view of the docked command-service module and the "Spider" LM. The earth can be seen in the background as astronaut Scott proceeds with his extravehicular activity.

A splendid view of the Apollo 9 lunar module, in a lunar landing configuration, as photographed from the command-service module on the fifth day of the mission. The LM "Spider" is flying upside down in relation to the earth below. "Spider's" landing gear has been deployed, and the lunar surface probes (sensors) extend out from the landing gear foot pads. Scott remained at the controls of "Gumdrop" while McDivitt and Schweickart were inside "Spider," checking out the craft.

Above, astronaut Schweickart is photographed from "Gumdrop" during his extra-vehicular activity. In his right hand, he is holding a thermal sample which he is retrieving from the LM exterior. Schweickart is standing in "golden slippers" — gold-painted restraints outside the threshold — on the lunar module porch. Below, bearded and smiling, the astronauts pause in front of the helicopter after pickup. They splashed down less than 5 miles from the recovery carrier *Guadalcanal* and 760 miles southeast of Cape Kennedy, having completed 151 earth orbits. It had been a textbook flight that had successfully verified the lunar module.

Seated before a model of the moon they will soon visit are the prime astronauts for the Apollo 10 flight. From left are Eugene A. Cernan, the LM pilot; Thomas P. Stafford, spacecraft commander; and John W. Young, command module pilot. All three are veterans of previous flights. Their mission is to provide additional experience in combined system operation during the three-day trip to the vicinity of the moon in lunar orbit. With the exception of actually landing on the moon in the LM, the mission plan is the same as the lunar landing mission itself.

On May 18, 1969, Apollo 10 rose slowly off the pad and swung into its eight-day mission. This now classic view of the command module was photographed by the crew of the lunar module (LM), after CSM-LM separation during lunar orbit. At this point the CSM was some 175 miles east of Smyth's Sea and above the rough terrain typical of the far side of the moon. Absence of shadows and bright craters indicates that the sun was almost directly overhead.

In this famous shot taken by astronaut John Young in Apollo 10's command module, the lunar module carrying Tom Stafford and Gene Cernan ascends from the moon to meet with the CM. The LM was nicknamed "Snoopy" and it came up from 8.4 nautical miles of the lunar surface to rendezvous with "Charlie Brown," the command module.

Above, one of the best crater shots photographed by the crew of Apollo 10 was this one showing a northwestward oblique view of Triesnecker Crater. It was taken from the CSM and shows terrain features typical of the northeastern Central Bay and the highlands along the northern margin of Central Bay. Below, Apollo 10 astronauts demonstrate weightlessness.

This memorable view of earth-rise over the lunar surface was taken after Apollo 10's transearth insertion. Darker maria (seas) contrast with the lighter highlands. Below, just before splashdown near Samoa in the South Pacific about four miles from the recovery ship *Princeton*, the astronauts' three chutes open against a South Pacific sunrise. A fantastically successful lunar orbital mission of 192 hours, this flight of Apollo 10 paved the way for the moon landing that was to occur only a few weeks hence.

The first men to set foot on the moon were Neil A. Armstrong (left) and Edwin E. ("Buzz") Aldrin, Jr. (extreme right). But no less a part of the prime astronaut crew of the famous Apollo 11 mission was Michael Collins (center), who was the command module pilot. On time to within less than a second, Apollo 11 blasted off from Launch Pad 39A at Cape Kennedy on July 16, 1969. Thus began what is looked upon as the greatest single step in human history — the much-fabled trip to the moon, with a manned landing and a return to earth. Watching intently was a worldwide TV audience — an estimated one million eyewitnesses.

When this spectacular photo of the earth was made, Apollo 11 was already about 98,000 miles from earth during its translunar coast toward the moon. Most of Africa and portions of Europe and Asia can be seen.

"They also serve. . . ." Gleeful Apollo 11 officials relax in the Launch Control Center following the successful lift-off of the moon-bound astronauts. From left to right are: Charles W. Mathews, Deputy Associate Administrator for Manned Space Flight; Dr. Wernher von Braun, Director of the Marshall Space Flight; and Lieutenant General Samuel C. Phillips, Director of the Apollo program. Below, this view of the rising earth greeted the Apollo 11 astronauts as they came from behind the moon after making their lunar orbit insertion burn.

Getting closer! The approach to the Apollo landing site is seen in this photo taken from the lunar module in lunar orbit. When this picture was made, the LM was still docked to the command and service modules, the shadow of which can be seen on the moon's surface. Site is located in the center of the photo near the edge of darkness. This view of the southwestern Sea of Tranquility looks in a generally westerly direction.

Footprint for history. After the LM settled down with a jolt on the lunar surface, Armstrong radioed Mission Control: "The Eagle has landed." It was 4:18 P.M. on July 20, 1969. A few hours later, at 10:56 P.M., Neil Armstrong put his left foot on the moon's surface. The first print made by the weight of a man on the moon is that of a lunar boot, which resembles an oversized galosh. For Armstrong's actual step-out on the lunar surface, see the Frontispiece of this book.

Astronaut "Buzz" Aldrin was the second man on the moon. Here he poses for a shot taken by Neil Armstrong beside the flag of the United States. Deployment of the flag by the two astronauts officially established Tranquility Base on the lunar surface. The flag itself measured 3 by 5 feet; its top edge had to be braced by a spring wire to keep it extended on the windless moon. Seven minutes after the planting of the flag on the lunar surface at 11:41 P.M., President Nixon talked to the two astronauts. "Neil and Buzz, I am talking to you from the Oval Room at the White House. . . ." The astronauts also left a commemorative plaque on the moon bearing the names of the crew members and President Nixon.

Above, Buzz Aldrin prepares to deploy the Early Apollo Scientific Experiments Package (EASEP) during his extravehicular activity. Below, Neil Armstrong took this picture of his fellow astronaut with a special lunar surface camera. Aldrin is approaching the leg of the landing craft during his EVA.

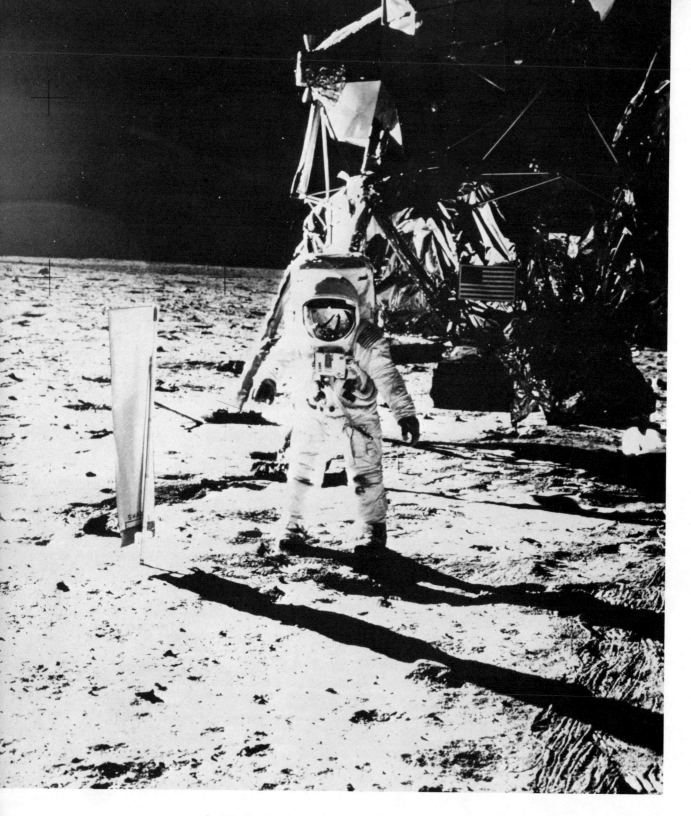

In this fine lunar photograph, Aldrin stands by the deployed Solar Wind Composition equipment. The device was used to collect particles of the "solar wind," or radiation, emanating from the sun. Other instrumentation left on the moon for scientific purposes included a seismic detector to record moonquakes, meteorite impact, or volcanic activity, and a laser reflector designed to make much more precise earth-moon measurements than ever before.

Homeward bound. This view of the Apollo 11 lunar module ascent stage was photographed by Michael Collins from the command service module during rendezvous
in lunar orbit. Astronauts Armstrong and Aldrin in the LM were making their docking approach to the CSM. Still on the lunar surface was the LM's descent stage,
which had been used as a launch platform. A rising earth can be seen above the
lunar horizon. With them on this ascent stage the astronauts are carrying the lunar
soil samples, the aluminum foil on which the "solar wind" particles have been
collected, and the flags and other mementos to be returned to earth. Largest item
left behind was the descent stage, that part of the landing craft with the plaque on
one of its spidery legs.

Above, these glass spherules of various colors and crystals were among the samples collected by astronauts Armstrong and Aldrin during the Apollo 11 lunar landing mission. The astronauts splashed down in the Pacific Ocean and recovery was made by the U.S.S. *Hornet* on July 24, 1969. Immediately quarantined in a mobile trailer unit, the astronauts were welcomed by President Nixon, who was visible to them through a window of the unit. Speaking over an intercom, the President greeted the astronauts, in part, with these words: "This is the greatest week in the history of the world since the Creation...." Below, a grateful Congress honored the Apollo 11 astronauts after their eight-day flight, as Buzz Aldrin, in his turn, addresses a joint meeting.

American astronauts selected to crew the nation's second manned lunar landing mission were (from left) Charles Conrad, Jr., spacecraft commander; Richard F. Gordon, command module pilot; and Alan L. Bean, lunar module pilot. Conrad and Gordon were both veterans of the Gemini 11 mission. But there was trouble during lift-off from Cape Kennedy on November 14. In a rainstorm, there was a momentary loss of the spacecraft's electrical power shortly after blastoff, due to a bolt of lightning. But power was soon restored and there was no apparent damage.

A revealing view of the now greatly sophisticated American spacecraft. This is Apollo 12 as it hovers above the instrument unit atop the mighty Saturn 5 launch vehicle just prior to the mating of the two. Lunar module's landing gear may be seen at the open end of the adapter, on top of which are mounted the Apollo service and command modules. The famed White Room, through which all astronauts enter their spacecraft, is attached to the mobile launcher's uppermost arm at left.

This shot taken by Lunar Orbiter 3 shows the planned landing area for Apollo 12. The landing ellipse, measuring some 7 by 3 nautical miles, is within a few hundred feet of Surveyor 3, an unmanned probe that had been soft-landed on the moon in April, 1967. In fact, the Apollo 12 astronauts touched down only about 600 feet from Surveyor 3 (see next page) on November 19, almost exactly at their aiming point on the Ocean of Storms.

Two U.S. spacecraft on the surface of the moon! This unusual photo, shot during the Apollo 12 extravehicular activity, shows the unmanned Surveyor 3 spacecraft in the foreground and, behind it in the background, the Apollo 12 lunar module. The TV camera and other gear were taken from the old Surveyor 3 and brought back to earth for scientific examination. Astronaut Gordon remained in the CSM in lunar orbit, while Conrad and Bean made the descent in the LM to explore the moon. Below, Alan Bean takes a core sample during his EVA on the surface of the moon. Note astronauts' footprints in the soft lunar soil in foreground.

The astronaut who took this picture on the Ocean of Storms is reflected in the face shield of his fellow crewman. The "faceless" astronaut above is holding a container of lunar soil collected during extravehicular activity. Note the checklist he wears on his left wrist to facilitate his preplanned work schedule.

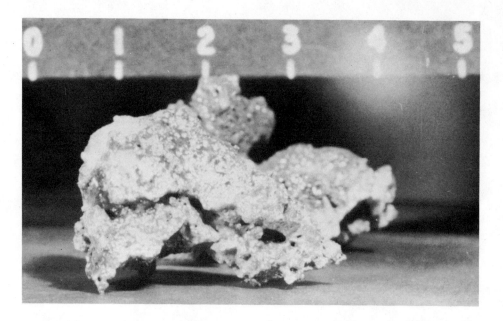

A rock from the moon. This sample from the lunar surface was collected by astronaut Alan Bean in a small crater about 1 meter across. It is tightly compacted, contains several pits, and is heavily coated with glass. It is a rock type known as breccia, composed of small fragments cemented together. Below, splashdown occurred on November 24, 1969, about 350 miles southeast of Samoa. Apollo's 10-day mission had been an outstanding success. The only flaw in the mission had been the failure of its color TV camera for 44 minutes of transmission on November 19. Below, the astronauts are seated in their life raft with respirators on as Navy pararescuemen close the hatch of the spacecraft during recovery operations. Once aboard the carrier *Hornet* and inside the Mobile Quarantine Facility, the astronauts removed their masks.

Members of the prime crew of the Apollo 13 lunar landing mission were (from left) astronauts James A. Lovell, Jr., Thomas K. Mattingly II, and Fred W. Haise, Jr. However, Mattingly, who had become exposed to German measles, could not make the mission and so backup astronaut John L. Swigert, Jr., was selected to go in Mattingly's place. The Apollo 13 flight was targeted to land in the Fra Mauro region of the moon, southeast of the Ocean of Storms, to conduct scientific experiments, to obtain more samples of the lunar surface, and to develop man's capability to work in the lunar environment.

The astronauts practice a moon walk (left) and picking up rock samples with special tongs (below). But it was a moon walk they would not take — at least not in Apollo 13. Although the astronauts lifted off successfully on April 11, 1970, for what was to have been the third lunar landing mission, the moon landing had to be aborted due to the explosion of one of the oxygen tanks in the service module.

Even though the moon landing was now impossible, Apollo 13 was committed to go into lunar orbit before making the burn that would send it back on the return journey to earth. It was a long, anxious, and grueling flight back. Short of oxygen and water, the Apollo 13 crewmen were forced to use the lunar module as a "lifeboat." Above is a view of the severely damaged service module. The service module was photographed from the lunar module/command module just after it was jettisoned. As is apparent here, an entire panel on the SM was blown away, presumably by oxygen tank number 2. The lunar module was jettisoned by the astronauts just prior to the command module's reentry into the earth's atmosphere.

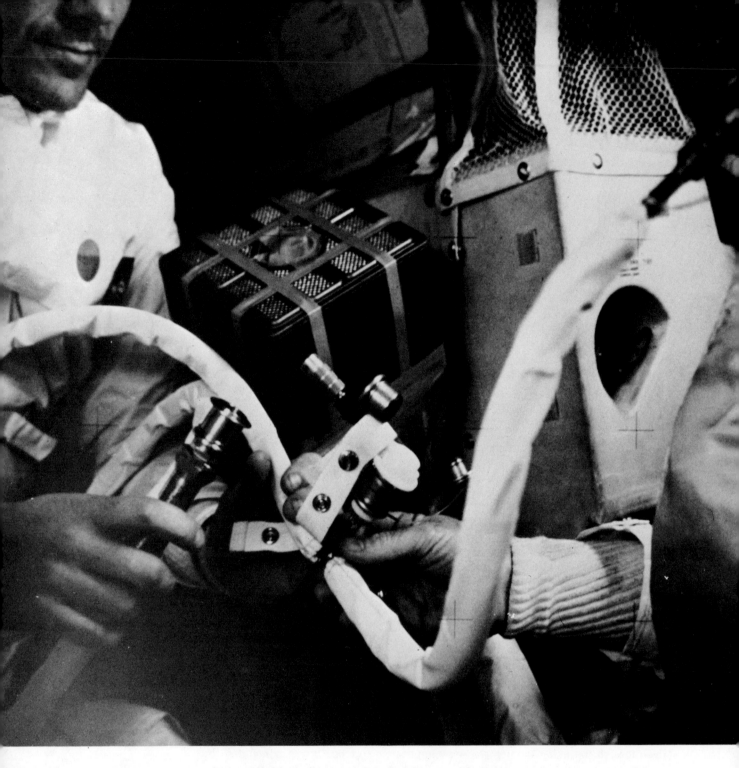

As an anxious world worried and prayed for the safety of the imperiled Apollo 13 crew, the astronauts aboard the crippled spacecraft were running short of a healthy air supply to breathe. Carbon dioxide was slowly building up in their lunar module "lifeboat." Here, John Swigert is holding the jerry-rigged arrangement which the astronauts built to purge the CO_2 from the LM. Called the "mailbox," it made use of the CM liphium hydroxide cannisters to "scrub" the CO_2 from the atmosphere of the spacecraft. Actually, the "mailbox" device was designed and tested on the ground at the Manned Spacecraft Center at Houston before it was suggested to the problem-plagued astronauts.

The perilous mission was concluded when the Apollo 13 astronauts splashed down in the Pacific Ocean at 12:07 P.M. John Swigert is being assisted into the net that will lift him to the waiting helicopter above. The mission commander, Jim Lovell, will be the last man to depart the life raft. Fred Haise is already aboard the chopper that will carry the astronauts to the waiting prime recovery ship, USS *Iwo Jima*.

The good air of earth! And the Apollo 13 astronauts breathe deeply of it aboard the flight deck of the carrier *Iwo Jima*. Thus did the grateful crewmen, Fred Haise (left), Jim Lovell, and John Swigert, write the finish to a space adventure in which the whole world had participated — if only vicariously. Congratulations poured in from all over the globe expressing the relief and joy of many nations at the safe return of three brave men. But these and other astronauts of NASA's bold and successful Project Apollo knew that Apollo was not yet finished. There would be other missions, other lunar landings.

BRIEF BIOGRAPHIES OF UNITED STATES ASTRONAUTS

(Alphabetically presented and compiled from Official NASA publications)

EDWIN E. ALDRIN, JR., was born in Montclair, New Jersey, January 20, 1930. He was graduated from the U.S. Military Academy in 1951 with a bachelor of science degree.

A member of the U.S. Air Force, Aldrin completed his pilot training at Bryan, Texas, in 1952. He flew combat missions during the Korean conflict; he also served a tour as aerial gunnery instructor at Nellis Air Force Base, Nevada, and attended Squadron Officers' School at the Air University, Maxwell Air Force Base, Alabama. Aldrin flew as a flight commander with the 36th Tactical Fighter Wing at Bitburg, Germany.

Aldrin completed work for his doctor of science degree in astronautics at Massachusetts Institute of Technology in 1963 and was assigned to the Gemini Target Office of the Air Force Space Systems Division, Los Angeles, California. He was later assigned to the Manned Spacecraft Center, Houston, Texas, to coordinate Department of Defense participation in Gemini experiments.

He was one of the fourteen astronauts selected by NASA in October, 1963. He was pilot of the back-up crew for the Gemini 9 mission and pilot for the Gemini 12 flight. He has received the NASA Exceptional Service Medal for his space flight achievements. A crew member of the famed Apollo 11 mission, Aldrin was the second man to set foot on the moon in 1969.

Aldrin is married to the former Joan A. Archer of Hohokus, New Jersey. They have three children.

JOSEPH P. ALLEN IV was born June 27, 1937, in Crawfordsville, Indiana. He received a bachelor of arts degree in math-physics from DePauw University in 1959, a master of science degree in physics from Yale University in 1962, and a doctorate in physics (nuclear physics) from Yale in 1965.

Allen was one of eleven scientist-astronauts selected by NASA in August, 1967. Prior to his selec-tion, Allen was a research associate at the University of Washington, Seattle.

He is married to the former Bonnie Jo Darling of Elkhart, Indiana. They have one child.

WILLIAM A. ANDERS was born in Hong Kong, October 17, 1933. He was graduated from the U.S. Naval Academy with a bachelor of science degree in 1955. After graduation, Anders was commissioned in the Air Force and received flight training. He received his master of science degree in nuclear engineering from the Air Force Institute of Technology, Wright-Patterson Air Force Base, Ohio. In 1962 he served as a nuclear engineer and instructor pilot at the Air Force Weapons Laboratory, Kirkland Air Force Base, New Mexico.

Anders was one of the fourteen astronauts selected by NASA in October, 1963. He was pilot of the backup crew for the Gemini II mission. In December, 1968, Anders was a crew member of the Apollo 8 lunar orbital mission.

Anders is married to the former Valerie E. Hoard of Lemon Grove, California. They have five children.

NEIL A. ARMSTRONG was born in Wapakoneta, Ohio, August 5, 1930. He graduated from Purdue University with a bachelor of science degree in aeronautical engineering in 1955.

Armstrong was a naval aviator from 1949 to 1952 and flew combat missions during the Korean conflict.

After graduation from Purdue University, Armstrong joined the NASA Lewis Flight Propulsion Laboratory and later transferred to NASA's High Speed Flight Station at Edwards Air Force Base, California. As an aeronautical research pilot, Armstrong was an X-15 project pilot flying that aircraft to over 200,000 feet and at approximately 4,000 miles per hour. Other flight test work included piloting the X-1 rocket research airplane, the F-100, the F-101, F-102, F-104, F5D, B-47, and the paraglider.

Armstrong was one of the nine astronauts selected by NASA in September, 1962. Armstrong was command pilot for the Gemini 8 mission flown March 16, 1966, and backup command pilot for the Gemini 5 and 11 missions.

As a member of the famed Apollo 11 lunar flight, Armstrong on July 20, 1969, became the first man to set foot on the moon.

He is the recipient of the 1962 Institute of Aeronautical Sciences Octave Chanute Award and the NASA Exceptional Service Award for his work in manned space flight.

In July, 1970, Armstrong was appointed Deputy Associate Administrator for Aeronautics for NASA.

Armstrong is married to the former Janet Shearon of Evanston, Illinois. They have two children.

CHARLES A. BASSETT II was named as an astronaut by NASA in October, 1963.

A major in the U.S. Air Force, he was born in Dayton, Ohio, December 30, 1931. Following graduate work in electrical engineering at the University of Southern California, he entered the military service in October, 1952.

Major Bassett lost his life in an aircraft accident during a routine flight to St. Louis, Missouri, on February 28, 1966.

ALAN L. BEAN, born in Wheeler, Texas, March 15, 1932, was graduated from the University of Texas in 1955 with a bachelor of science degree in aeronautical engineering.

After graduation, Bean was commissioned in the U.S. Navy. He received pilot training and was assigned to Attack Squadron 44 at Jacksonville Naval Station for four years. He then attended the Navy Test Pilot School at Patuxent, Maryland, and served as project officer there on various aircraft for Navy preliminary evaluation, initial trials, and final board of inspections and survey trials. Bean's last Navy assignment was with Attack Squadron 172 at Cecil Field, Florida.

Bean was selected by NASA as one of fourteen chosen in October, 1963. He was the command pilot for the backup crew for the Gemini 10 mission. In November, 1969, Alan Bean was a crew member of the Apollo 12 lunar landing mission, during which he performed EVA on the moon's surface.

He is married to the former Sue Ragsdale of Dallas, Texas. The Beans have two children.

FRANK BORMAN was born in Gary, Indiana, March 14, 1928. Raised in Tucson, Arizona, he graduated from the U.S. Military Academy in 1950 with a bachelor of science degree.

After receiving pilot training at Williams Air Force Base, Arizona, he was assigned to various fighter squadrons in the United States and the Philippines. In 1957 he became an instructor in thermodynamics and fluid mechanics at the military academy.

Borman received a master's degree in aeronautical engineering from California Institute of Technology in 1957. He was graduated from the USAF Aerospace Research Pilots School in 1960 and remained there as an instructor until 1962.

Borman was one of the nine astronauts selected by NASA in September, 1962. He was command pilot for the Gemini 7 mission, which established a number of records, including the longest manned space flight performed up to that time (330 hours and 35 minutes). He participated in the first rendezvous of two manned maneuverable spacecraft (Gemini 7 and Gemini 9) on December 15, 1965. In December, 1968, Frank Borman participated in the Apollo 8 lunar orbital mission.

Borman has been awarded the NASA Exceptional Service Award and was co-recipient of the 1966 Harmon International Aviation Trophy for his space flight achievements.

He is married to the former Susan Bugbee of Tucson, Arizona. The Bormans have two children.

VANCE D. BRAND was born in Longmont, Colorado, May 9, 1931. He received a bachelor of science degree in business administration from the University of Colorado in 1953, and a bachelor of science degree in aeronautical engineering from the same university in 1960. Brand received a master's degree in business administration from the University of California at Los Angeles in 1964.

He served with the U.S. Marine Corps as a commissioned officer from 1953 to 1957. Brand completed naval flight training in 1955 and subsequently was designated a naval aviator and served a fifteen-month tour of duty in Japan as a jet fighter pilot.

Brand was one of the nineteen astronauts selected by NASA in April, 1966. Prior to his selection, he was assigned as an engineering test pilot for Lockheed Aircraft Corporation at the West German F-104G Flight Test Center at Istres, France. He worked for Lockheed from 1960 to 1966 and was employed initially as a flight test engineer. He later attended the U.S. Naval Test Pilot School at Patuxent River, Maryland, as a civilian under Lockheed sponsorship.

He is married to the former Joan Virginia Weninger of Chicago, Illinois. The Brands have four children.

M. SCOTT CARPENTER was born in Boulder, Colorado, May 1, 1925. After World War II he entered the University of Colorado and received a bachelor of science degree in aeronautical engineering.

Carpenter participated in the V-5 flight training program sponsored by the U.S. Navy at the University of Colorado in 1943.

Carpenter was one of the seven astronauts selected by NASA in April, 1959. He served as backup pilot to John Glenn on the Mercury-Atlas 6 flight. Carpenter commanded the MA-7 three-orbit flight on May 24, 1962, and was awarded the NASA Distinguished Service Medal for his space voyage. Later he resigned from the astronaut program to return to the Navy and pursue his interest in deep-sea exploration.

He is married to the former Rene Louise Price of Clinton, Iowa. The Carpenters have four children.

GERALD P. CARR was born in Denver, Colorado, August 22, 1932. He received a bachelor of science degree in mechanical engineering from the University of Southern California in 1954; a bachelor of science degree in aeronautical engineering from the U.S. Naval Postgraduate School in 1961; and a master of science degree in aeronautical engineering from Princeton University in 1962.

He entered the U.S. Navy in 1949. Upon his graduation from the University of Southern California in 1954, he received his commission in the Marine Corps. He received flight training at Pensacola, Florida, and Kingsville, Texas. He was then assigned to Marine All-Weather Fighter Squadron 114. From 1962 to 1965, he served with Marine All-Weather Fighter Squadron 122 in the United States and the Far East. His last assignment prior to his selection as an astronaut was with the Test Directors Section, Marine Air Control Squadron 3, a unit responsible for carrying out testing and evaluation of Marine tactical data systems.

Carr was one of the nineteen astronauts selected by NASA in April, 1966.

He is married to the former JoAnn Ruth Petrie of Santa Ana, California. The Carrs have six children.

EUGENE A. CERNAN was born in Chicago, Illinois, March 14, 1934. He was graduated from Purdue University in 1956 with a bachelor of science degree in electrical engineering.

Cernan was commissioned by the U.S. Navy after completing the Navy Reserve Officer Training Corps program at Purdue and entered flight training. He was assigned to Attack Squadrons 126 and 113 at Miramar, California, Naval Air Station. In 1961, Cernan entered the U.S. Naval Postgraduate School at Monterey, California, where he received a master of science degree in aeronautical engineering.

Cernan was one of the fourteen astronauts selected by NASA in October, 1963. Cernan was pilot for the Gemini 9 mission launched June 3, 1966, and performed a two hour and seven minute space walk (extravehicular activity). He was pilot of the backup crew for Gemini 12.

He received the NASA Exceptional Service Medal for his space flight accomplishments during the Gemini 9 mission. In May of 1969, Cernan participated in the eight-day Apollo 10 lunar orbital mission.

Cernan is married to the former Barbara J. Atchley of Houston, Texas. They have one daughter.

ROGER B. CHAFFEE was named an astronaut by NASA in October, 1963.

He was born in Grand Rapids, Michigan, February 15, 1935. He graduated from Purdue University with a bachelor of science degree in aeronautical engineering in 1957. Joining the Navy later that year, he rose to the rank of lieutenant commander.

Commander Chaffee met death while participating in a simulated countdown of an Apollo spacecraft on January 27, 1967.

PHILIP K. CHAPMAN was born March 5, 1935, in Melbourne, Australia. Chapman became a U.S. citizen on May 8, 1967. He received a bachelor of science degree in physics from Sydney University (Australia) in 1956, and a master of science degree in aeronautics and astronautics from Massachusetts Institute of Technology (M.I.T.) in 1964. He received his doctorate in physics (instrumentations) from M.I.T. in 1967.

Chapman was an auroral/radio physicist with the Antarctic Division, External Affairs Department, Commonwealth of Australia from 1957 through 1959. He was with the Australia National Antarctic Research Expedition, IGY, in 1958. In 1960 and 1961 Chapman was a staff engineer in electro-optics with Canadian Aviation Electronics, Dorval, Quebec. Prior to his selection as a scientist-astronaut he was a staff physicist in the Experimental Astronomy Laboratory at M.I.T.

Chapman was one of eleven scientist-astronauts selected by NASA in August, 1967.

Married to the former Pamela Gatenby of Herberton, Queensland, the Chapmans have one child.

MICHAEL COLLINS was born in Rome, Italy, October 31, 1930. He attended the U.S. Military Academy and was graduated in 1952 with a bachelor of science degree.

After graduation, Collins was commissioned by the U.S. Air Force and served as an experimental flight test officer at the Air Force Flight Test Center, Edwards Air Force Base, California. He tested performance, stability, and control characteristics of Air Force aircraft, primarily jet fighters.

Collins was one of fourteen astronauts selected by NASA in October, 1963. He served as backup pilot for the Gemini 7 mission. He was pilot of the prime crew for Gemini 10 launched July 18, 1966, and during that mission Collins proved man's capability for performing extravehicular tasks relative to a target vehicle. He performed three separate periods of extravehicular activity during this flight.

He received the NASA Exceptional Service Medal for his accomplishments on the Gemini 10 mission.

In July, 1969, Collins was a crew member of the famed Apollo 11 lunar landing mission, during which he piloted the command module.

Collins is married to the former Patricia M. Finnegan of Boston, Massachusetts. They have three children. Collins resigned from NASA in December, 1969.

CHARLES CONRAD, JR., was born in Philadelphia, Pennsylvania, June 2, 1930. He was graduated from Princeton University in 1953 with a bachelor of science degree in aeronautical engineering.

He entered the Navy following his graduation from Princeton. Conrad attended the Navy Test Pilot School at Patuxent River, Maryland, and following completion of that course was a project test pilot in the Armaments Test Division there. He also served at Patuxent as a flight instructor and performance engineer. Just prior to his selection as an astronaut, Conrad served as safety officer for Fighter Squadron 96 at the Naval Air Station, Miramar, California.

Conrad was one of nine astronauts selected by NASA in September, 1962. Conrad was pilot on the Gemini 5 endurance mission launched from Cape Kennedy on August 21, 1965. He was backup command pilot for the Gemini 8 mission and command pilot on Gemini 11 launched September 12, 1966.

He was awarded the NASA Exceptional Service Medals for his Gemini 5 and 11 space flight accomplishments.

In 1969, Conrad participated in the Apollo 12 lunar landing mission, during which he performed EVA with Alan Bean on the surface of the moon.

Conrad is married to the former Jane DuBose of Uvalde, Texas. They have four children.

L. GORDON COOPER, JR., was born March 6, 1927, in Shawnee, Oklahoma. He was graduated from the Air Force Institute of Technology, Wright-Patterson Air Force Base, Ohio, in 1956 with a bachelor of science degree in aeronautical engineering.

Cooper entered the U.S. Marine Corps in 1945 and later attended the Naval Academy Preparatory School. He was a member of the Presidential Honor Guard in Washington until his discharge in August, 1946. Cooper entered the University of Hawaii, Hono-

lulu, and received an Army commission after attending for three years. He transferred this commission to the Air Force and entered flight training in 1949. Upon completion of this training, Cooper flew with the 86th Fighter Bomber Group in Munich, Germany, for four years. After graduating from the Air Force Institute in 1956, he was assigned to the Air Force Experimental Flight Test School at Edwards Air Force Base, California.

Cooper, one of seven astronauts selected in April, 1959, on May 15, 1963, piloted MA-9 spacecraft on a 22-orbit mission. Cooper was command pilot for the Gemini 5 flight launched from Cape Kennedy, August 21, 1965. He was also assigned as command pilot of the backup crew for Gemini 12.

He has been awarded the NASA Distinguished Service Medal and the NASA Exceptional Service Medal.

Cooper is married to the former Trudy Olson of Seattle, Washington. They have two daughters.

ROBERT L. CRIPPEN, born in Beaumont, Texas, on September 11, 1937, was graduated from New Caney High School in New Caney, Texas, and in 1960 received a bachelor of science degree in Aerospace Engineering from the University of Texas.

Crippen received his commission through the Navy's Aviation Officer Program at Pensacola, Florida, which he entered after graduation from the University of Texas. He continued his flight training at Whiting Field, Florida, and went from there to Chase Field in Beeville, Texas, where he received his wings. From June, 1962, to November, 1964, he was assigned to Fleet Squadron VA-72, completing two and one-half years of duty as an attack pilot aboard the aircraft carrier U.S.S. *Independence*. He later attended the USAF Aerospace Research Pilot School at Edwards Air Force Base, California, and, upon graduation, remained there as an instructor until his selection in October, 1966, to the USAF Manned Orbiting Laboratory Program. Crippen was among the second group of aerospace research pilots to be assigned to the MOL program.

Crippen became a NASA astronaut in September, 1969. He is currently involved in training for future manned space flights.

Crippen is married to the former Virginia E. Hill. They have three children.

R. WALTER CUNNINGHAM was born March 16, 1932, in Creston, Iowa. Reared in Venice, California, he received a bachelor of arts degree in physics from the University of California at Los Angeles (UCLA) in 1960 and a master of arts degree in physics in 1961 from that same university.

Cunningham joined the U.S. Navy in 1951 and entered flight training in 1952. He was assigned to a Marine squadron in 1953 and remains a Marine reservist.

Prior to his selection as an astronaut, Cunningham was with the Rand Corporation where he worked as a research scientist. He performed error analysis and feasibility studies of defense against submarine-launched ballistic missiles and problems of the earth's magnetosphere. His later work at UCLA was developing, testing, and analyzing results of a tri-axial search coil magnetometer which was flown aboard the first NASA Orbiting Geophysical Observatory satellite.

Cunningham was one of the fourteen astronauts selected by NASA in October, 1963. In October, 1968, he participated in the Apollo 7 rendezvous and simulated docking mission.

He is married to the former Lo Ella Irby of Norwalk, California. The Cunninghams have two children.

CHARLES M. DUKE, JR., was born in Charlotte, North Carolina, October 3, 1935. He received a bachelor of science degree from the U.S. Naval Academy in 1957 and a master of science degree in aeronautics and astronautics from the Massachusetts Institute of Technology in 1964.

He was commissioned in the U.S. Air Force in 1957, upon graduation from the naval academy. He completed flight training in 1958 and was later assigned to the 526th Fighter Interceptor Squadron at Ramstein, Germany, where he served three years as a fighter-interceptor pilot. His last assignment prior to his selection as an astronaut was as instructor in control systems at the Air Force Aerospace Research Pilot School, from which he graduated in 1965.

Duke was one of the nineteen astronauts selected by NASA in April, 1966.

He is married to the former Dorothy Meade Claiborne of Atlanta, Georgia. The Dukes have two children.

DONN F. EISELE was born in Columbus, Ohio, June 23, 1930. He received a bachelor of science degree from the U.S. Naval Academy in 1952 and in 1960 he received a master of science degree in astronautics from the Air Force Institute of Technology at Wright-Patterson Air Force Base, Ohio.

After graduation from the U.S. Naval Academy, Eisele chose the U.S. Air Force as a career. He completed flight training and later was graduated from the Air Force Aerospace Research Pilot School, Edwards Air Force Base, California. He served as project engineer and experimental test pilot at the Air Force Special Weapons Center, Kirtland Air Force Base, New Mexico. He flew experimental and developmental test flights in jet aircraft in support of special weapons developmental programs.

Eisele was one of the fourteen astronauts selected by NASA in October, 1963. In October, 1968, he participated in the Apollo 7 rendezvous and simulated docking mission.

He is married to the former Harriet E. Hamilton of Gnaddenhutten, Ohio, and the Eiseles have four children.

ANTHONY W. ENGLAND was born May 15, 1942, in Indianapolis, Indiana. He received a bachelor of science degree in geology and physics from the Massachusetts Institute of Technology (M.I.T.) in 1965, a master of science degree in geology and physics from M.I.T. in 1965, and a doctorate in geophysics from M.I.T. in 1967.

England was one of eleven scientist-astronauts selected by NASA in August, 1967.

Prior to his selection, England was a graduate fellow at M.I.T.

He is married to the former Kathleen Ann Kreutz of Fargo, North Dakota. They have one child.

JOE H. ENGLE was born in Abilene, Kansas, August 26, 1932. He received a bachelor of science degree in aeronautical engineering from the University of Kansas in 1955.

He was commissioned in the U.S. Air Force through the Reserve Officer Training Corps program at the University of Kansas and entered flying school in 1957. Upon completion of flight training, he served with the 474th Fighter Day Squadron and the 309th Tactical Fighter Squadron at George Air Force Base, California. He had assignments in Spain, Italy, and Denmark. In 1961, Engle was graduated from the Experimental Flight Test Pilot School and from the Air Force Aerospace Research Pilot School in 1962. His last assignment prior to being selected as an astronaut was as an areospace flight test pilot in the X-15 research program at Edwards Air Force Base, California.

Engle was one of the nineteen astronauts selected by NASA in April, 1966.

He is married to the former Mary Catherine Lawrence of Mission Hills, Kansas. They have two children.

RONALD E. EVANS was born in St. Francis, Kansas, November 10, 1933. He received a bachelor of science degree in electrical engineering from the University of Kansas in 1956, and a master of science degree in aeronautical engineering from the U.S. Naval Postgraduate School in 1964.

He was commissioned through the Reserve Officer

Training Corps program and completed flight training in 1957. He had carrier duty with two cruises and was assigned to Fighter Squadron 124 in 1961 and 1962, where he served as combat flight instructor on F8 aircraft. His last assignment prior to being selected as an astronaut was on carrier duty flying F8 aircraft in Vietnam combat operations.

Evans was one of the nineteen astronauts selected by NASA in April, 1966.

Evans is married to the former Janet Merle Pollom of Topeka, Kansas. They have two children.

THEODORE C. FREEMAN was named an astronaut by NASA in October, 1963.

A captain, U.S. Air Force, Freeman was born in Haverford, Pennsylvania, February 18, 1930. A graduate of the U.S. Naval Academy, Freeman received his master of science degree from Michigan University in 1960.

Captain Freeman died in an aircraft accident during a routine test flight at Ellington Air Force Base, October 31, 1964.

CHARLES G. FULLERTON was born October 11, 1936, in Rochester, New York. He was graduated from U.S. Grant High School in Portland, Oregon, and received from the California Institute of Technology bachelor of science and master of science degrees in Mechanical Engineering in 1957 and 1958, respectively.

Fullerton received primary and basic flight training at Bainbridge Air Base, Georgia, and Webb Air Force Base, Texas. He entered active duty with the Air Force in July, 1958, after having worked as a mechanical design engineer for the Hughes Aircraft Company in Culver City, California. He went to Perrin Air Force Base, Texas, in September, 1959, for F-86 fighter interceptor training and was then assigned from May to December, 1960, at McConnell Air Force Base, Kansas, for B-47 combat crew training. Following completion of this training, he served as a B-47 jet bomber pilot with Strategic Air Command's 303rd Bomb Wing at Davis Monthan Air Force Base, Arizona. After graduation in May, 1965, from the USAF Aerospace Research Pilot School at Edwards Air Force Base, California, he reported to the Aeronautical Systems Division at Wright-Patterson Air Force Base, Ohio. He was a test pilot for the bomber operations division at Wright-Patterson when notified of his selection to the USAF Manned Laboratory Program as a flight crew member.

Fullerton became a NASA astronaut in September, 1969. He is currently involved in training for future manned space flights.

He is married to the former Marie J. Buettner of Delphos, Ohio.

OWEN K. GARRIOTT was born November 22, 1930, in Enid, Oklahoma. He was graduated from the University of Oklahoma in 1953 with a bachelor's degree in electrical engineering. He was graduated from Stanford University, Stanford, California, in 1957 with a master's degree in electrical engineering. He received his doctorate from Stanford in 1960.

Garriott was a consultant to the Manned Space Science Division of NASA's Office of Space Sciences and Applications. He was consultant to the Lockheed Corporation's Space Physics branch. Garriott has served as secretary to the U.S. Commission, International Scientific Radio Union, and was regional editor of *Planetary and Space Sciences*. From 1961 until 1965, Garriott taught electronics, electromagnetic theory, and ionospheric physics at Stanford University and has performed research in ionospheric physics since obtaining his doctorate at Stanford.

Garriott was one of the six scientist-astronauts selected by NASA in June, 1965. He completed flight training at Williams Air Force Base, Arizona, in 1966.

He is married to the former Helen Mary Walker of Enid, Oklahoma. The Garriotts have four children.

EDWARD G. GIBSON was born November 8, 1936, in Buffalo, New York. He was graduated from the University of Rochester, New York, with a bachelor of science degree and from the California Institute of Technology with a master of science degree. He received his doctorate in engineering physics from the California Institute of Technology in June, 1964.

Gibson was a research assistant specializing in jet propulsion and atmospheric physics while studying at the California Institute of Technology. He also wrote several technical papers, including some on his work with lasers. After receiving his doctorate, Gibson did aerospace research with the Philco Corporation's Applied Research Laboratories, Newport Beach, California.

Gibson was one of the six scientist-astronauts selected by NASA in June, 1965. He completed flight training at Williams Air Force Base, Arizona, in 1966.

He is married to the former Julia Ann Volk of the Township of Tonawanda, New York. The Gibsons have two children.

EDWARD G. GIVENS, JR. was one of the nineteen astronauts selected by NASA in April, 1966.

Major Givens was born in Quanah, Texas, January 5, 1930. He received a bachelor of science degree from the U.S. Naval Academy in 1952.

Prior to his selection as an astronaut, he had been assigned to the Air Force's Space Systems Division Office at the Manned Spacecraft Center, Houston, Texas.

Major Givens lost his life in an off-duty automobile accident on June 6, 1967.

JOHN H. GLENN was born July 18, 1921, in Cambridge, Ohio, and attended Muskingum College at Concord, Ohio. Entering the Naval Aviation Cadet Program in 1942, he was commissioned in the Marine Corps in 1943.

In April, 1959, he was selected as an astronaut for Project Mercury. As pilot of "Friendship 7" spacecraft, Glenn was the first American to make an orbital flight. Launched from Cape Kennedy, Florida, the flight reached a maximum altitude of 162 miles and made 3 orbits in 4 hours, 55 minutes, 23 seconds, before landing in the Atlantic Ocean near Grand Turk Island.

Awarded the Distinguished Flying Cross five times, Glenn also holds the Air Medal with eighteen clusters. He retired from the astronaut program in 1964 and became a consultant to NASA's administrator in February, 1965.

His wife is the former Anna Margaret Castor. They have two children.

RICHARD F. GORDON, JR., was born in Seattle, Washington, October 5, 1929. He received his bachelor of science degree in chemistry from the University of Washington in 1951.

Gordon entered the U.S. Navy in 1951 and received his naval aviator wings in 1953. He attended All-Weather Flight School and received jet transitional training before reporting to an all-weather squadron at the Naval Air Station, Jacksonville, Florida. Gordon attended the Navy's Test Pilot School at Patuxent River, Maryland, in 1957, and serving as a flight test pilot, was the first project test pilot for the F4H Phanton II.

In May, 1961, Gordon won the Bendix Trophy Race from Los Angeles, California, to New York, establishing a new speed record of 869.74 mph and a transcontinental record of 2 hours and 47 minutes.

Gordon was one of the fourteen astronauts selected by NASA in October, 1963. Gordon was pilot of the backup crew for the Gemini 8 flight and pilot of the prime crew for the Gemini 11 mission launched September 12, 1966. He was awarded the NASA Exceptional Service Medal for his accomplishments on that flight.

In November, 1969, Gordon participated in the Apollo 12 lunar landing mission, during which he piloted the command module in lunar orbit.

He is married to the former Barbara Field of Seattle, Washington. The Gordons have six children.

VIRGIL I. GRISSOM was pilot of the Mercury-Redstone 4 (Liberty Bell 7) suborbital mission, July 21, 1961, which attained an altitude of 118 miles and traveled 302 miles in 15 minutes and 37 seconds. He was also commander of Gemini 3, a three-orbit mission flown on March 23, 1965.

A lieutenant colonel in the U.S. Air Force, Grissom was born in Mitchell, Indiana, April 3, 1926, and named astronaut by NASA April, 1959.

He met death during a simulated countdown of an Apollo spacecraft, January 27, 1967.

FRED W. HAISE, JR., was born in Biloxi, Mississippi, November 14, 1933. He received a bachelor of science degree in aeronautical engineering from the University of Okahoma in 1959.

He served with the U.S. Navy, beginning in 1952, and was assigned as a U.S. Marine Corps fighter pilot from 1954 to 1956. From 1957 to 1959, he was a fighter-interceptor pilot with the Oklahoma Air National Guard. He served with the Air Force in 1961 and 1962 and was awarded the A. B. Honts Trophy as the outstanding graduate from the Aerospace Research Pilot School in 1964.

Haise was one of the nineteen astronauts selected by NASA in April, 1966. Prior to his selection, he was a research pilot at the NASA Flight Research Center at Edwards, California. From September, 1959, to March, 1963, he was a research pilot at the NASA Lewis Research Center in Cleveland, Ohio.

In April, 1970, Haise was aboard the Apollo 13 spacecraft, whose lunar landing mission had to be aborted due to an explosion in the service module.

Haise is married to the former Mary Griffin Grant of Biloxi, Mississippi. They have four children.

KARL G. HENIZE was born October 17, 1926, in Cincinnati, Ohio. He received a bachelor of arts degree in mathematics from the University of Virginia in 1947, and a master of arts degree in astronomy from the University of Virginia in 1948. In 1954 Henize received his doctorate in astronomy from the University of Michigan.

Henize was a Carnegie fellow at Mount Wilson Observatory from 1954 to 1956, and a senior astronomer at the Smithsonian Astrophysical Observatory from 1956 to 1959. Prior to his selection as a scientist-astronaut he was a professor of astronomy at Northwestern University.

Henize was one of eleven scientist-astronauts selected by NASA in August, 1967.

He is married to the former Caroline Rose Weber of Bay City, Michigan. They have three children.

DONALD L. HOLMQUEST was born April 7, 1939, in Dallas, Texas. He received a bachelor of science degree in electrical engineering from Southern Methodist University in 1962. He received his M.D. from Baylor College of Medicine in 1967. Prior to his selection as a scientist-astronaut, Holmquest was working on his doctorate in physiology at the Baylor College of Medicine. He received his degree in 1968. He has also completed his internship at Methodist Hospital in Houston, Texas.

Holmquest was one of eleven scientist-astronauts selected by NASA in August, 1967.

He is married to the former Charlotte Ann Blaha of Dallas, Texas. They have no children.

JAMES B. IRWIN was born in Pittsburgh, Pennsylvania, on March 17, 1930. He received a bachelor of science degree from the U.S. Naval Academy in 1951 and a master of science degree in aeronautical engineering and instrumentation engineering from the University of Michigan in 1957.

He was commissioned in the U.S. Air Force in 1951 and received flight training at Hondo Air Base, Texas, and Reese Air Force Base, Texas. Irwin has served with the F-12 Test Force at Edwards Air Force Base, California, and the AIM 47 Project Office at Wright-Patterson Air Force Base, Ohio. He graduated from the Air Force Experimental Flight Test Pilot School in 1961, and from the Air Force Aerospace Research Pilot School in 1963. His last assignment prior to his selection as an astronaut was as chief of the Advanced Requirements Branch at Headquarters Air Defense Command.

Irwin was one of the nineteen astronauts selected by NASA in April, 1966.

He is married to the former Mary Ellen Monroe of Corvallis, Oregon. The Irwins have four children.

JOSEPH P. KERWIN was born in Oak Park, Illinois, February 19, 1932. He was graduated from the College of the Holy Cross, Worcester, Massachusetts, with a bachelor of arts degree. Kerwin received his doctor of medicine degree from the Northwestern University Medical School, Chicago, Illinois, and completed his internship at the District of Columbia General Hospital, Washington, D.C., and at the U.S. Navy School of Aviation Medicine, Pensacola, Florida.

Kerwin entered the U.S. Navy in 1958. He completed flight training at Beeville, Texas, in 1962, and was named the outstanding student in his preflight class. Kerwin served two years as flight surgeon with Marine Air Group 14 at Cherry Point, North Carolina.

He later served as flight surgeon for Fighter Squadron 101 at Oceana Naval Air Station, Virginia Beach, Virginia; he then became staff flight surgeon for Air Wing 4, Naval Air Station, Cecil Field, Florida.

Kerwin was one of the six scientist-astronauts selected by NASA in June, 1965.

He is married to the former Shirley Good of Danville, Pennsylvania. The Kerwins have two children.

WILLIAM B. LENOIR was born March 14, 1939, in Miami, Florida. He received a bachelor of science degree in electrical engineering from the Massachusetts Institute of Technology in 1961, a master of science degree in electrical engineering from M.I.T. in 1962, and a doctorate in electrical engineering from M.I.T. in 1965.

Lenoir was one of eleven scientist-astronauts selected by NASA in August, 1967.

Prior to his selection, Lenoir was an assistant professor of electrical engineering at M.I.T.

He is married to the former Elizabeth May Frost of Brookline, Massachusetts. They have one child.

DON L. LIND was born in Murray, Utah, May 18, 1930. He received a bachelor of science degree in physics from the University of Utah in 1953, and a doctor of philosophy degree in high energy nuclear physics from the University of California in 1964.

He served with the U.S. Navy on active status from 1954 to 1957. Lind completed his flight training in 1955 and was subsequently assigned to carrier duty.

Lind was one of the nineteen astronauts selected by NASA in April, 1966. Prior to his selection, Lind worked at the NASA Goddard Space Flight Center as a space physicist, where he was involved in experiments to determine the nature and properties of low energy particles within the earth's magnetosphere and interplanetary space. Before 1964, he was employed at the Lawrence Radiation Laboratory, Berkeley, California, doing research in pion-nucleon scattering.

He is married to the former Kathleen Maughan of Logan, Utah. The Linds have five children.

JACK R. LOUSMA was born in Grand Rapids, Michigan, on February 29, 1936. He received a bachelor of science degree in aeronautical engineering from the University of Michigan in 1959 and the degree of "Aeronautical Engineer" from the U.S. Naval Postgraduate School in 1965.

He entered the U.S. Marine Corps in 1959 and completed flight training in 1960 at the U.S. Naval Air Training Command. He was assigned as an attack pilot and subsequently served in Iwakuni, Japan.

Lousma's last assignment before his selection as an astronaut was as a reconnaissance pilot at the Marine Air Station, Cherry Point, North Carolina.

Lousma was one of the nineteen astronauts selected by NASA in April, 1966.

He is married to the former Gratia Kay Smeltzer of Ann Arbor, Michigan. The Lousmas have two children.

JAMES A. LOVELL, JR., was born March 25, 1928, at Cleveland, Ohio. He received a bachelor of science degree from the U.S. Naval Academy in 1952.

Lovell received flight training following graduation from the academy. He served in a number of assignments including a four-year tour as a test pilot at the Naval Air Test Center at Patuxent River, Maryland. He was program manager for the F4H weapon system evaluation. Lovell was graduated from the Aviation Safety School at the University of Southern California and served as flight instructor and safety officer with Fighter Squadron 101 at the Naval Air Station, Oceana, Virginia.

Lovell was one of the nine astronauts selected by NASA in September, 1962. He was pilot of the Gemini 7 mission, which was launched on December 4, 1965, and splashed down after 330 hours and 35 minutes. Lovell served as backup pilot for the Gemini 4 mission, backup command pilot for Gemini 9, and command pilot for the Gemini 12 mission.

He has received the NASA Exceptional Service Medal for his space flight achievements; the 1966 Harmon International Trophy; and the 1966 American Astronautical Society Achievement Award.

In April of 1970, Jim Lovell was designated mission commander of the Apollo 13 lunar landing flight, during which the moon touchdown was aborted due to an explosion in the service module.

Lovell is married to the former Marilyn Gerlach of Milwaukee, Wisconsin. They have four children.

BRUCE McCANDLESS II was born in Boston, Massachusetts, June 8, 1937. He received a bachelor of science degree from the U.S. Naval Academy in 1958; a master of science degree in electrical engineering from Stanford University in 1965; and is working toward a doctor of philosophy degree in electrical engineering at Stanford University.

He was graduated second in his class from the naval academy and received flight training at Pensacola, Florida, and Kingsville, Texas. In 1960 he received weapons system and carrier landing training at Key West, Florida. From 1960 to 1964 McCandless was assigned to Fighter Squadron 102 and participated in carrier duty, including the Cuban blockade. In early 1964 he was instrument flight instructor in Attack Squadron 43 at Naval Air Station Apollo

Soucek Field, Oceana, Virginia. His assignment before his selection as an astronaut was at Stanford University doing graduate studies in electrical engineering.

McCandless was one of the nineteen astronauts selected by NASA in April, 1966.

McCandless is married to the former Bernice Doyle of Rahway, New Jersey. They have two chidren.

JAMES A. McDIVITT was born in Chicago, Illinois, June 10, 1929. He was graduated from the University of Michigan with a bachelor of science degree in aeronautical engineering in 1959, first in his class. He received an honorary doctor of philosophy degree in astronautical science from the University of Michigan in 1965.

He joined the Air Force in 1951 and during the Korean War flew 145 combat missions. He is a graduate of the U.S. Air Force Experimental Test Pilot School and the U.S. Air Force Aerospace Research Pilot School. He served at Edwards Air Force Base, California, as an experimental test pilot.

McDivitt was one of the nine astronauts selected by NASA in September, 1962. He was command pilot for the Gemini 4 mission, which was a 66-orbit, 4-day mission, launched from Cape Kennedy June 3, 1965.

He received the NASA Exceptional Service Award for his flight. Among other aeronautic and space-related awards, McDivitt has received the Arnold Air Society John Fitzgerald Kennedy Award for 1966.

In March, 1969, McDivitt was mission commander of the Apollo 9 earth orbital exercises to test the lunar excursion module. McDivitt is presently manager, Apollo Spacecraft office, Houston, Texas.

He is married to the former Patricia A. Haas of Cleveland, Ohio. The McDivitts have four children.

THOMAS K. MATTINGLY II was born in Chicago, Illinois, March 17, 1936. He received a bachelor of science degree in aeronautical engineering from Auburn University in 1958.

He entered the U.S. Navy in 1958 and completed flight training in 1960. From 1960 to 1963 he was assigned to Attack Squadron 35 and flew A1H aircraft on carrier duty. In 1963 he served in A3B aircraft, also on carriers. His last assignment prior to his selection as an astronaut was as a student at the Air Force Aerospace Research Pilot School.

Mattingly was one of the nineteen astronauts selected by NASA in April, 1966.

Selected as one of the prime crew members of the Apollo 13 mission, Mattingly had been exposed to German measles and was replaced by another astronaut.

Mattingly is not married.

EDGAR D. MITCHELL was born in Hereford, Texas, September 17, 1930. He received a bachelor of science degree in industrial management from the Carnegie Institute of Technology in 1952, a bachelor of science degree in aeronautical engineering from the U.S. Naval Postgraduate School in 1961, and a doctor of science degree in aeronautics/astronautics from the Massachusetts Institute of Technology in 1964.

Mitchell entered the Navy in 1952, was commissioned in 1953, completed flight training in 1954, and was assigned to Patrol Squadron 29 in Okinawa. In 1957 and 1958 he flew A3 aircraft as part of Heavy Attack Squadron 2 on carrier duty. He was a research project officer with Air Development Squadron 5 in 1958 and 1959. After receiving his doctorate in 1964, he was assigned as Chief, Project Management Division, at the Navy Field Office for Manned Orbiting Laboratory. Prior to his selection as an astronaut, he graduated first in his class at the Air Force Aerospace Research Pilot School.

Mitchell was one of the nineteen astronauts selected by NASA in April, 1966.

He is married to the former Louise Elizabeth Randall of Muskegon, Michigan. The Mitchells have two daughters.

F. STORY MUSGRAVE was born August 19, 1935, in Boston, Massachusetts. Musgrave has earned the following college degrees: a bachelor of science degree in statistics from Syracuse University in 1958; a masters degree in business administration in operations analysis from UCLA in 1959; a bachelor of arts degree in chemistry from Marietta College in 1960; an M.D. from Columbia University in 1964; a master of science degree in biophysics from the University of Kentucky in 1966; and a doctorate in physiology from the University of Kentucky in 1967.

Musgrave was one of eleven scientist-astronauts selected by NASA in August, 1967.

Prior to his selection, Musgrave was a post-doctoral fellow at the University of Kentucky.

He is married to the former Marguerite Patricia Van Kirk of Wayne, New Jersey.

ROBERT F. OVERMYER was born July 14, 1936, in Lorain, Ohio. He attended schools in Westlake, Ohio, and received a bachelor of science degree in physics from Baldwin-Wallace College in 1958 and a master of science degree in aeronautics from the U.S. Naval Postgraduate School in 1964.

Overmyer entered active duty with the U.S. Marine Corps in January, 1958. His participation during the preceding summer in a twelve-week platoon leaders' course at Quantico, Virginia, qualified him for a

second lieutenant's commission upon completion of college in December, 1957. He received naval flight training at Pensacola, Florida, and Kingsville, Texas, and was assigned in October, 1959, to VMA-214 (Marine Attack Squadron). Following this tour of duty at the Marine Corps Air Station in Kaneohe Bay, Hawaii, Overmyer attended the U.S. Naval Postgraduate School in Monterey, California. He graduated in June, 1964, and was then assigned to MAMS-17 (Marine Aircraft Maintenance Squadron) in Iwakuni, Japan. From August, 1965, to August, 1966, he was a student at the USAF Aerospace Research Pilot School at Edwards Air Force Base, California; and upon graduation, was selected for participation in the USAF Manned Orbiting Laboratory Program as a crew member.

Overmeyer became a NASA astronaut in September, 1969. He is currently involved in training for future space flights.

He is married to the former Katherine E. Jones of Pittsburgh, Pennsylvania. The Overmyers have 2 children.

ROBERT A. PARKER was born December 14, 1936, in New York City, New York. He received a bachelor of arts degree in astronomy and physics from Amherst College in 1958, and a doctorate in astronomy from the California Institute of Technology in 1963.

Parker was one of eleven scientist-astronauts selected by NASA in August, 1967.

Prior to his selection, Park was an assistant professor of astronomy at the University of Wisconsin.

He is married to the former Joan Audrey Capers of Waynesboro, Pennsylvania. They have two children.

WILLIAM R. POGUE was born in Okemah, Oklahoma, January 23, 1930. He received a bachelor of science degree in education from Oklahoma Baptist University in 1951, and a master of science degree in mathematics from Oklahoma State University in 1960.

He entered the Air Force in 1951 and received his commission in 1952. He served with the Fifth Air Force in 1953 and 1954 and flew 43 combat missions over Korea. From 1955 to 1957 he was a member of the USAF Thunderbirds. Pogue has gained flying proficiency in over fifty types and models of American and British aircraft and is qualified as a civilian flight instructor. From 1960 to 1963, he served as mathematics instructor at the USAF Academy in Colorado Springs, Colorado. He is a graduate of the Empire Test Pilots' School in Farnborough, England, and in 1965 he completed a two-year tour as test pilot with the British Ministry of Aviation under the USAF/RAF Exchange Program. Prior to his selection as an astronaut, he was an instructor at the Air Force Aerospace Research Pilot School, Edwards Air Force Base, California.

Pogue was one of the nineteen astronauts selected by NASA in April, 1966.

He is married to the former Helen J. Dittmar of Shawnee, Oklahoma. The Pogues have three children.

STUART A. ROOSA was born in Durango, Colorado, August 16, 1933. He received a bachelor of science degree in aeronautical engineering from the University of Colorado in 1960.

Roosa entered the U.S. Air Force in 1953, and was commissioned in the Air Force after graduation from the Aviation Cadet Program at Williams Air Force Base, Arizona. He flew F-84F and F-100 aircraft during a tour of duty at Langley Air Force Base, Virginia. After graduation from the University of Colorado under the Air Force Institute of Technology Program, he was chief of Service Engineering at Tachikawa Air Base, Japan, for two years.

From 1962 to 1964, Roosa was a maintenance test pilot at Olmsted Air Force Base, Pennsylvania. He graduated from the Air Force Aerospace Research Pilot School in 1965 and was assigned as an experimental test pilot at Edwards Air Force Base, California, prior to his selection as an astronaut.

Roosa was one of the nineteen astronauts selected by NASA in April, 1966.

He is married to the former Joan C. Barrett of Tupelo, Mississippi. The Roosas have four children.

WALTER M. SCHIRRA, JR., was born in Hackensack, New Jersey, March 12, 1923. He received a bachelor of science degree from the U.S. Naval Academy in 1945 and an honorary doctorate in astronautical engineering from Lafayette College, Pennsylvania, in 1966.

He received flight training at Pensacola, Florida. During the Korean conflict, Schirra flew 90 combat missions. Other assignments include project pilot for the F7U3 Cutlass and instructor pilot for the Cutlass and FJ3 Fury; operations officer on a carrier in the Pacific; test pilot training; and suitability development work on the F4H.

Schirra was one of the seven astronauts selected by NASA in April, 1959. He was pilot of Project Mercury Sigma 7 six-orbit "textbook" flight on October 3, 1962, and command pilot of Gemini 6, December 15–16, 1965, which established a space "first" by performing rendezvous with Gemini 7.

The veteran astronaut added to his laurels in October, 1968, when he commanded the Apollo 7 ten-day 163-orbit mission.

He received the NASA Distinguished Service Medal twice and the Exceptional Service Medal once. Other awards include: American Rocket Society Astronautics Award, 1963; Collier Trophy, 1963; American Institute of Aeronautics and Astronautics Award, 1963; American Astronautical Society Flight Achievement Award, 1966; and the 1966 Harmon International Aviation Trophy.

Schirra is married to the former Josephine Fraser of Seattle, Washington. They have two children.

HARRISON H. SCHMITT was born in Santa Rita, New Mexico, July 3, 1935. He received his bachelor of science degree in geology from the California Institute of Technology in 1957. He attended the University of Oslo in Norway, 1957 and 1958, and received his doctorate in geology at Harvard University in 1964. Schmitt has been awarded a Fulbright Fellowship, 1957–58; a Kennecott Fellowship in Geology, 1958–59; a Harvard Fellowship, 1959–60; a Harvard Traveling Fellowship, 1960; a Parker Traveling Fellowship, 1961–62; and a National Science Foundation Postdoctoral Fellowship, Department of Geological Sciences, Harvard University, 1963–64.

He has done geological work for the Norwegian Geological Survey in Oslo, and for the U.S. Geological Survey in New Mexico and Montana. Prior to his selection as an astronaut, Schmitt was with the U.S. Geological Survey's Astrogeology Department at Flagstaff, Arizona. He was project chief on photo and telescopic mapping of the moon and planets, and was among the USGS astrogeologists instructing NASA astronauts during their geological field trips.

Schmitt was one of the six scientist-astronauts selected by NASA in June, 1965. He finished flight training in 1966.

Schmitt is not married.

RUSSELL L. SCHWEICKART was born in Neptune, New Jersey, October 25, 1935. He received a bachelor of science degree in aeronautical engineering in 1956 and a master of science degree in aeronautics and astronautics in 1963 from Massachusetts Institute of Technology (M.I.T.). His thesis was on stratospheric radiance.

He served as a pilot in the U.S. Air Force from 1956 to 1960. He was recalled to active duty for a year in 1961. Prior to his selection as an astronaut he was a research scientist at the Experimental Astronomy Laboratory at M.I.T. His duties there included research in upper atmospheric physics and applied astronomy, as well as research in star tracking and stabilization of stellar images.

Schweickart was one of the fourteen astronauts selected by NASA in October, 1963.

In March, 1969, Russell Schweickart was aboard as a crew member of the Apollo 9 mission performing valuable work in the testing of the lunar module phase of Project Apollo.

He is married to the former Clare G. Whitfield of Atlanta, Georgia. The Schweickarts have five children.

DAVID R. SCOTT was born in San Antonio, Texas, June 6, 1932. He received a bachelor of science degree from the U.S. Military Academy in 1954, graduating fifth in a class of 633. From 1960 to 1962 he attended Massachusetts Institute of Technology (M.I.T.) and earned both a master of science degree in aeronautics and astronautics and an engineer of aeronautics and astronautics degree. His thesis at M.I.T. concerned interplanetary navigation.

As an Air Force officer, after his graduation from the military academy, he received flight training, attended the Air Force Experimental Test Pilot School, and the Air Force Aerospace Research Pilot School.

Scott was one of the fourteen astronauts selected by NASA in October, 1963. He was pilot of the Gemini 8 flight, March 16, 1966. This flight marked the first successful docking of a spacecraft with a target vehicle in space.

He has been awarded the NASA Exceptional Service Medal and the American Institute of Aeronautics and Astronautics Award in 1966.

As an astronaut aboard Apollo 9 in March, 1969, Scott was assigned the duties of command module pilot.

Scott is married to the former Ann Lurton Ott of San Antonio, Texas. They have two children.

ELLIOT M. SEE, JR., was named as an astronaut by NASA in September, 1962.

Born in Dallas, Texas, July 23, 1927, he obtained his master's degree in engineering from the University of California in 1962.

Mr. See served three years in the Navy and was employed as a test pilot for ten years by the General Electric Company.

See lost his life in an aircraft accident during a routine flight to St. Louis, Missouri, on February 28, 1966.

ALAN B. SHEPARD, JR., was born in East Derry, New Hampshire, November 18, 1923. He received a bachelor of science degree from the U.S. Naval Academy in 1944.

Following destroyer service in the Pacific in World War II, he entered flight training and received his wings in 1947. Shepard's assignments in the Navy

include U.S. Navy Test Pilot School at Patuxent River, Maryland, and flight test work there. He participated in experiments in development of the Navy's in-flight refueling system; carrier trials for the F2H3; Navy trials of the first angled carrier deck; testing of the F3H, F8U, F4D, F11F; and project test pilot on the F5D. He was graduated from the Naval War College, Newport, Rhode Island, in 1958 and was assigned to the staff of the commander in chief, Atlantic Fleet, as air readiness officer.

Shepard was one of the seven astronauts selected by NASA in April, 1959, and is now Chief, Astronaut Office. On May 5, 1961, he was this country's first man in space as pilot of the Mercury-Redstone 3, a suborbital flight. The flight attained an altitude of approximately 116 statute miles and the spacecraft traveled about 302 statute miles down the Eastern Test Range.

Shepard was awarded the NASA Distinguished Service Medal in 1961, and the Langley Medal in 1964.

He is married to the former Louise Brewer of Kennett Square, Pennsylvania. They have two children.

DONALD K. SLAYTON was born in Sparta, Wisconsin, March 1, 1924. He received a bachelor of science degree in aeronautical engineering from the University of Minnesota in 1949, and an honorary doctorate in engineering from Michigan Technological University in 1965.

He entered the U.S. Air Force in 1942 and became a pilot in 1943. During World War II he flew 56 combat missions in B-25's over southern Europe and seven combat missions over Japan. From 1949 to 1951, he worked as an aeronautical engineer for the Boeing Company in Seattle, Washington, until being recalled to active duty and assignment to 12th Air Force Headquarters. In 1955, Slayton attended the Air Force Flight Test Pilot School at Edwards Air Force Base, California. From 1956 to 1959, he was an experimental test pilot at that base.

Slayton was one of the seven astronauts selected by NASA in April, 1959. On November 29, 1961, he was named as the pilot of MA-7, the second manned orbital mission. On March 15, 1962, it was announced that a heart condition would prevent Slayton from making the flight. In November, 1963, he resigned his commission as Air Force major and continued with NASA Manned Spacecraft Center in the dual role of astronaut and Director, Flight Crew Operations, Houston, Texas.

Slayton was awarded the NASA Distinguished Service Medal in 1965.

He is married to the former Marjorie Lunney of Los Angeles, California. They have one son.

THOMAS P. STAFFORD was born in Weatherford, Oklahoma, September 17, 1930. He received a bachelor of science degree from the U.S. Naval Academy in 1952.

He was commissioned in the Air Force and completed flight training and advanced intercepter training. He served five years as a fighter-interceptor pilot and subsequently was graduated from the Air Force Experimental Flight Test School in 1959. He is coauthor of *Pilot's Handbook for Performance Flight Testing* and *Aerodynamics Handbook for Performance Flight Testing.*

Stafford was one of the nine astronauts selected by NASA in September, 1962. On December 15–16, 1965, with astronaut Walter M. Schirra, Jr., as command pilot, he was pilot of the Gemini 6 flight, which established a space "first" by achieving rendezvous with the orbiting Gemini 7. Stafford was command pilot of the Gemini 9 mission on June 3, 1966, during which pilot Eugene A. Cernan spent 2 hours and 7 minutes in extravehicular activity, and multiple rendezvous was achieved using three different techniques.

Stafford has twice been awarded the NASA Exceptional Service Medal and received the American Astronautical Society Flight Achievement Award in 1966. He was also awarded the 1966 Harmon International Aviation Trophy.

In May, 1969, Thomas Stafford commanded the eight-day Apollo 10 mission, the "dress rehearsal" for the actual lunar landing.

He is married to the former Faye L. Shoemaker of Weatherford, Oklahoma. They have two children.

JOHN L. SWIGERT was born in Denver, Colorado, August 30, 1931. He received a bachelor of science degree in mechanical engineering from the University of Colorado in 1953 and a master of science degree in aerospace science from the Rensselaer Polytechnic Institute in 1965, and a master of science degree in business administration from the University of Hartford in 1967.

He served with the U.S. Air Force from 1953 to 1956. After completing flight training, Swigert was assigned as a fighter pilot in Japan and Korea.

Swigert was one of the nineteen astronauts selected by NASA in April, 1966. Prior to his selection, he was an engineering test pilot for North American Aviation, Inc., from 1964 to 1966. Swigert was co-recipient of the AIAA Octave Chanute Award for 1966 for his participation in demonstrating the Rogallo Wing as a feasible land landing system for returning space vehicles and astronauts. From 1957 to 1964 he was a research engineering test pilot for Pratt and Whitney Aircraft.

Swigert, in April, 1970, participated in the Apollo 13 flight, which was aborted on its intended lunar landing mission due to an explosion in the command module.

Swigert is not married.

WILLIAM E. THORNTON was born April 14, 1929, in Goldsboro, North Carolina. He received a bachelor of science degree in physics from the University of North Carolina in 1952, and an M.D. degree from the University of North Carolina in 1963.

Thornton was the director of the Electronics Division, Del Mar Engineering Labs, Los Angeles, from 1956 to 1962. He was an instructor at the University of North Carolina Medical School in 1963 and 1964. In 1964 and 1965 Thornton was an intern at Wilford Hall USAF Hospital, Lackland Air Force Base, San Antonio, Texas. From 1965 to 1967 Thornton was associated with the Aerospace Medical Division, Brooks Air Force Base, San Antonio, Texas.

Thornton was one of eleven scientist-astronauts selected by NASA in August, 1967.

He is married to the former Elizabeth Jennifer Fowler of Great Britain. They have two children.

RICHARD H. TRULY was born in Fayette, Mississippi, on November 12, 1937. He attended schools in Fayette and Meridian, Mississippi and received a bachelor of aeronautical engineering degree from Georgia Institute of Technology in 1959.

Truly received his commission through the Naval Reserve Officer Training Corps (NROTC) program at Georgia Tech. He completed naval flight training in 1960 at Beeville, Texas, and was assigned to Fighter Squadron 33 from 1960 to 1963. During this period, he served aboard the U.S.S. *Intrepid* and the U.S.S. *Enterprise.* He was a member of Class 64A at the USAF Aerospace Research Pilot School, Edwards Air Force Base, California, and was subsequently assigned there as an instructor upon graduation. From November, 1965, to September, 1969, he was assigned to the USAF Manned Orbiting Laboratory Program on astronaut status. Truly became a NASA astronaut in September, 1969. He is currently involved in training for future manned space flights.

He is married to the former Colleen Hanner of Milledgeville, Georgia. The Trulys have three children.

PAUL J. WEITZ was born in Erie, Pennsylvania, July 25, 1932. He received a bachelor of science degree in aeronautical engineering from Pennsylvania State University in 1954 and a master of science degree from the U.S. Naval Postgraduate School in 1964.

He received his Navy commission through the Reserve Officer Training Corps at Pennsylvania State University and was assigned to destroyer duty in 1954. He completed flight training in 1956. From 1956 to 1960 he was assigned to the Naval Air Station in Jacksonville, Florida, as tactics instructor. From 1960 to 1962 Weitz served as project officer for various air-to-ground delivery tactics projects at China Lake, California. Prior to his selection as an astronaut, he was a detachment officer-in-charge at the Naval Air Station at Whidbey, Washington.

Weitz was one of the nineteen astronauts selected by NASA in April, 1966.

Weitz is married to the former Suzanne M. Berry of Erie, Pennsylvania. They have two children.

EDWARD H. WHITE, pilot for the four-day Gemini mission in June, 1965, was the first American to "walk" in space. He spent twenty-one minutes outside the spacecraft during the flight's third orbit.

Born in San Antonio, Texas, November 14, 1930, he was a graduate of the U.S. Military Academy and rose to a lieutenant colonel in the U.S. Air Force. He was named as an astronaut by NASA in September, 1962.

Ed White met death while participating in a simulated countdown of an Apollo spacecraft mission on January 27, 1967.

CLIFTON C. WILLIAMS, JR., was one of the fourteen astronauts selected by NASA in October, 1963.

He was born in Mobile, Alabama, September 26, 1932, and received his bachelor of science degree in mechanical engineering from Auburn University in 1954.

Williams was a graduate of the Navy Test Pilot School at Patuxent, Maryland. At the time of his selection as an astronaut, he was attending the Marine Corps Intermediate Staff and Command School at Quantico, Virginia.

Astronaut Williams lost his life in the crash of his T-38 jet trainer on October 6, 1967.

ALFRED M. WORDEN was born in Jackson, Michigan, February 7, 1932. He received a bachelor of science degree from the U.S. Military Academy in 1955 and master of science degree in astronautical/aeronautical engineering and instrumentation engineering from the University of Michigan in 1963.

He was commissioned in the Air Force after graduation from the military academy and completed flight training in Texas and Florida. From 1957 to 1961 he served as pilot and armament officer with the 95th Fighter Interceptor Squadron at Andrews Air Force Base, Maryland. He attended Instrument Pilots Instructor School at Randolph Air Force Base, Texas, in 1963. He was graduated from the Empire Test Pilots' School in Farnborough, England, in 1965, and from the Aerospace Research Pilots' School in 1965. When he was selected as an astronaut, he was assigned as an instructor at the Aerospace Research Pilot School.

Worden was one of the nineteen astronauts selected by NASA in April, 1966.

He is married to the former Pamela Ellen Vander Beek of Bayside, New York. The Wordens have two children.

JOHN W. YOUNG was born in San Francisco, California, September 24, 1930. He received a bachelor of science degree in aeronautical engineering from Georgia Institute of Technology in 1952.

Young entered the U.S. Navy in 1952. From 1959 to 1962 he served as a test pilot and program manager of the F4H weapons system project. In 1962 Young set world time-to-climb records in the 3,000-meter and 25,00-meter altitudes in the F4B navy fighter. He also served with Fighter Squadron 143 at Miramar, California.

He was one of the nine astronauts selected by NASA in September, 1962. He was pilot of the first manned Gemini flight, Gemini 3, on March 23, 1965, with astronaut Virgil I. Grissom as command pilot. This was a three-orbit mission in which the flight crew performed the first orbital maneuver conducted by man. He was selected as backup pilot for the Gemini 6 mission. Young was command pilot of the Gemini 10 mission. Among Gemini 10's accomplishments were dual rendezvous with two Agena target vehicles, combined maneuvering of Gemini/Agena X, space flight to 475 miles above the earth, and three periods of extravehicular activity by the pilot.

Young was awarded the NASA Exceptional Service Medal in 1965 and in 1966.

In May, 1969, this veteran astronaut participated in the lunar orbital mission of Apollo 10, serving as the pilot of the command/service module.

He is married to the former Barbara V. White of Savannah, Georgia. The Youngs have two children.

A GLOSSARY OF SPACE TERMS

Ablation. The removal of surface material from a body by vaporization, melting, or other process; specifically the intentional removal of material from a nose cone or spacecraft during high-speed movement through a planetary atmosphere to provide thermal protection to the underlying structure.

Abort. To cancel or cut short a flight.

Acceleration. The rate of change of velocity. Decrease in velocity is sometimes called negative acceleration.

Accumulator. A device or apparatus that accumulates or stores up, as: (a) a contrivance in a hydraulic system that stores fluid under pressure; (b) a device sometimes incorporated in the fuel system of a gas-turbine engine to store up and release fuel under pressure as an aid in starting.

Acquisition. 1. The process of locating the orbit of a satellite or trajectory of a space probe so that tracking or telemetry data can be gathered. 2. The process of pointing an antenna or telescope so that it is properly oriented to allow gathering of tracking or telemetry data from a satellite or space probe.

Acquisition and tracking radar. A radar set that locks onto a strong signal and tracks the object reflecting the signal.

Active. Transmitting a signal, as "active satellite," in contrast to "passive."

Aerobiology. The study of the distribution of living organisms freely suspended in the atmosphere.

Aerodynamic heating. The heating of a body produced by passage of air or other gases over the body, significant chiefly at high speeds, caused by friction and by compression processes.

Aerodynamics. The science that treats of the motion of air and other gaseous fluids, and of the forces acting on bodies when the bodies move through such fluids, or when such fluids move against or around the bodies, as "his research in aerodynamics."

Aerodynamic vehicle. A device, such as an airplane, glider, etc., capable of flight only within a sensible atmosphere and relying on aerodynamic forces to maintain flight. This term is used when the context calls for discrimination from "space vehicle."

Aeroembolism. 1. The formation or liberation of gases in the blood vessels of the body, as brought on by a change from a high, or relatively high, atmospheric pressure to a lower one. 2. The disease or condition caused by the formation or liberation of gases in the body. The disease is characterized principally by neuralgic pains, cramps, and swelling, and sometimes results in death. Also called decompression sickness.

Aerospace. (From *aero*nautics and *space*.) Of or pertaining to both the earth's atmosphere and space, as in "aerospace industries."

Aerospace medicine. That branch of medicine dealing with the effects of flight through the atmosphere or in space upon the human body, and with the prevention or cure of physiological or psychological malfunctions arising from these effects.

Air breakup. The breakup of a vehicle after reentry into the atmosphere. Air breakup is sometimes provided for, as by the firing of a cartridge inside the reentry body, so as to retard the fall of certain pieces and increase the chance of their recovery.

Air shower. A grouping of cosmic-ray particles observed in the atmosphere.

Anoxia. A complete lack of oxygen available for physiological use within the body. Compare hypoxia.

Apogee. In an orbit about the earth, the point at which the satellite is farthest from the earth; the highest altitude reached by a sounding rocket.

Apogee rocket. A rocket attached to a satellite or spacecraft designed to fire when the craft is at apogee, the point farthest from the earth in orbit. The effect of the apogee rocket is to establish a new orbit farther from the earth or to allow the craft to escape from earth orbit.

Artificial gravity. A simulated gravity established within a space vehicle, as by rotating a cabin about an axis of a spacecraft, the centrifugal force generated being similar to the force of gravity.

Astro. A prefix meaning "star" or "stars" and, by extension, sometimes used as the equivalent of "celestial," as in *astro*nautics.

Astrobiology. The study of living organisms on celestial bodies other than the earth.

Astrodynamics. The practical application of celestial mechanics, astroballistics, propulsion theory, and allied fields to the problem of planning and directing the trajectories of space vehicles.

Astronaut. 1. A person who occupies a space vehicle. 2. Specifically one of the test pilots selected to participate in Projects Mercury, Gemini, and Apollo, the United States programs for manned space flight.

Astronautics. 1. The art, skill, or activity of operating space vehicles. 2. In a broader sense, the science of space flight.

Atmosphere. The envelope of air surrounding the earth; also the body of gases surrounding or comprising any planet or other celestial body.

Attitude. The position or orientation of an aircraft, spacecraft, etc., either in motion or at rest, as determined by the relationship between its axes and some reference line or plane such as the horizon.

Backout. An undoing of things already done during a countdown, usually in reverse order.

Backup. 1. An item kept available to replace an item which fails to perform satisfactorily. 2. An item under development intended to perform the same general function performed by another item also under development.

Balloon-type rocket. A rocket, such as Atlas, that requires the pressure of its propellants (or other gases) within it to give it structural integrity.

Beam. A ray or collection of focused rays of radiated energy. Radio waves used as a navigation aid.

Beam-rider. A craft following a beam, particularly one which does so automatically, the beam providing the guidance.

"Bird." A colloquial term for a rocket, satellite, or spacecraft.

Blackout. 1. A fadeout of radio communications due to environmental factors such as ionospheric disturbances, or a plasma sheath surrounding a re-entry vehicle. 2. A condition in which vision is temporarily obscured by a blackness, accompanied by a dullness of certain of the other senses, brought on by decreased blood pressure in the head and a consequent lack of oxygen, as may occur in pulling out of a high-speed dive in an airplane.

Blockhouse. A reinforced concrete structure, often built underground or partly underground, and sometimes dome-shaped, to provide protection against blast, heat, or explosion during rocket launchings or related activities; specifically, such a structure at a launch site that houses electronic control instruments used in launching a rocket.

Boiloff. The vaporization of a cold propellant such as liquid oxygen or liquid hydrogen, as the temperature of the propellant mass rises as in the tank of a rocket being readied for launch.

Booster. Short for "booster engine" or "booster rocket."

Booster engine. An engine, especially a booster rocket, that adds its thrust to the sustainer engine.

Booster rocket. 1. A rocket engine, either solid or liquid fuel, that assists the normal propulsive system or sustainer engine of a rocket or aeronautical vehicle in some phase of its flight. 2. A rocket used to set a missile vehicle in motion before another engine takes over. In sense 2 the term "launch vehicle" is more commonly used.

Breakoff phenomenon. The feeling which sometimes occurs during the high altitude flight of being totally separated and detached from the earth and human society. Also called breakaway phenomenon.

Burn. A period during which a rocket engine is firing, as in "second burn," the second period during a flight in which the engine is firing.

Burnout. 1. An act or instance of the end of fuel and oxidizer burning in a rocket; the time at which this burnout occurs. Compare cutoff. 2. An act or instance of something burning out or of overheating; specifically, an act or instance of a rocket combustion chamber, nozzle, or other part overheating so as to result in damage or destruction.

Capsule. I. A boxlike component or unit, often sealed. 2. A small, sealed, pressurized cabin with an internal environment which will support life in a man or animal during extremely high altitude flight, space flight, or emergency escape.

Centrifuge. Specifically, a large motor-driven apparatus with a long arm at the end of which human and animal subjects or equipment can be revolved and rotated at various speeds to simulate very closely the prolonged accelerations encountered in high-performance aircraft, rockets, and spacecraft.

Checkout. A sequence of actions taken to test or examine a launch vehicle or spacecraft as to its readiness to perform its intended function.

Chemical fuel. 1. A fuel that depends upon an oxidizer for combustion or for development of thrust, such as liquid or solid rocket fuel or internal-combustion-engine fuel; distinguished from nuclear fuel. 2. A fuel that uses special chemicals, such as a boron-based fuel.

Chemical rocket. A rocket using chemical fuel — fuel which requires an oxidizer for combustion, such as liquid or solid rocket fuel.

Cislunar. (Latin cis, meaning "on this side.") Of or pertaining to phenomena, projects, or activity in the space between the earth and moon, or between the earth and the moon's orbit.

Closed ecological system. A system that provides for the maintenance of life in an isolated living chamber such as a spacecraft cabin by means of a cycle wherein exhaled carbon dioxide, urine, and other waste matter are converted chemically or by photosynthesis into oxygen, water, and food.

Companion body. A nose cone, last-stage rocket, or other body that orbits along with an earth satellite.

Complex. Entire area of launch site facilities. This includes blockhouse, launch pad, gantry, etc. Also referred to as a "launch complex."

Composite propellant. A solid rocket propellant consisting of a fuel and an oxidizer.

Computer. A machine for carrying out calculations and performing specified transformations on information.

Console. An array of controls and indicators for the monitoring and control of a particular sequence of actions, as in the checkout of a rocket, a countdown action, or a launch procedure. A console is usually designed around desklike arrays. It permits the operator to monitor and control different activating instruments, data recording instruments, or event sequencers.

Control. Specifically, to direct the movements of an aircraft, rocket, or spacecraft with particular reference to changes in altitude and speed.

Control rocket. A vernier engine, retrorocket, or other such rocket, used to guide or make small changes in the velocity of a rocket, spacecraft, or the like.

Cosmic dust. Small meteoroids of a size similar to dust.

Cosmic rays. The extremely high energy subatomic particles which bombard the atmosphere from outer space. Cosmic-ray primaries seem to be mostly protons, hydrogen nuclei, but also comprise heavier nuclei. On colliding with atmospheric particles they produce many different kinds of lower-energy secondary cosmic relation.

Countdown. The time period in which a sequence of events is carried out to launch a rocket; the sequence of events.

Cutoff. An act or instance of shutting something off; specifically in rocketry, an act or instance of shutting off the propellant flow in a rocket, or of stopping the combustion of the propellant.

Debug. 1. To isolate and remove malfunctions from a device or mistakes from a computer routine or program. 2. Specifically, in electronic manufacturing, to operate equipment under specified environmental and test conditions in order to eliminate failures and to stabilize equipment prior to actual use.

Deceleration. The act or process of moving, or of causing to move, with decreasing speed; the state of so moving.

Deep space net. A combination of three radar and communications stations in the United States, Australia, and South Africa, so located as to keep a spacecraft in deep space under observation at all times.

Deep space probes. Spacecraft designed for exploring space to the vicinity of the moon and beyond. Deep space probes with specific missions may be referred to as "lunar probe," "Mars probe," "solar probe," etc.

Destruct. The deliberate action of destroying a rocket vehicle after it has been launched, but before it has completed its course. Destructs are executed when the rocket gets off its plotted course or functions in a way so as to become a hazard.

Dish. A parabolic type of radio or radar antenna, roughly the shape of a soup bowl.

Docking. The process of bringing two spacecraft together while in space.

Drogue parachute. A type of parachute attached to a body, used to slow it down; also called deceleration parachute, or drag parachute.

Eccentric. Not having the same center; varying from a circle, as in "eccentric orbit."

Ecological system. A habitable environment, either created artificially, such as in a manned space vehicle, or occuring naturally, such as the environment on the surface of the earth, in which man, animals, or other organisms can live in mutual relationship with each other. Ideally, the environment furnishes the sustenance for life, and the resulting waste products revert or cycle back into the environment to be used again for the continuous support of life.

Ejection capsule. 1. In an aircraft or manned spacecraft, the detachable compartment serving as a cockpit or cabin, which may be ejected as a unit and parachuted to the ground. 2. In an artificial satellite, probe, or unmanned spacecraft, a boxlike unit usually containing recording instruments or records of observed data, which may be ejected and returned to earth by a parachute or other deceleration device.

Electromagnetic radiation. Energy propagated through space or through material media in the form of an advancing disturbance in electrical and magnetic fields existing in space or in the media. Also simply called radiation.

Escape velocity. The radial speed which a particle or larger body must attain in order to escape from the gravitational field of a planet or star. The escape velocity from earth is approximately 7 miles per second; from Mars, 3.2 miles per second; and from the sun, 390 miles per second.

Exobiology. The study of living organisms existing on celestial bodies other than the earth.

Extraterrestrial. From outside the earth.

Eyeballs in, eyeballs out. Terminology used by test pilots to describe the acceleration experienced by the person being accelerated. Thus the acceleration experienced by an astronaut at lift-off is "eyeballs in" (positive g in terms of vehicle acceleration), and the acceleration experienced when retrorockets fire is "eyeballs out" (negative 8 in terms of vehicle acceleration).

Fallaway section. A section of a rocket vehicle that is cast off and separates from the vehicle during flight, especially such a section that falls back to the earth.

Fatigue. A weakening or deterioration of metal or other material, or of a member, occurring under load, especially under repeated, cyclic, or continued loading.

Fixed satellite. An earth satellite that orbits from west to east at such a speed as to remain constantly over a given place on the earth's equator.

Free fall. 1. The fall or drop of a body, such as a rocket not guided, not under thrust, and not retarded by a parachute or other braking device. 2. Weightlessness.

g or G. An acceleration equal to the acceleration of gravity, approximately 32.2 feet per second per second at sea level; used as a unit of stress measurement for bodies undergoing acceleration.

Gantry. A frame structure that spans over something, as an elevated platform that runs astride a work area, supported by wheels on each side; specifically, short for "gantry crane" or "gantry scaffold."

Gantry scaffold. A massive scaffolding structure mounted on a bridge or platform supported by a pair of towers or trestles that normally run back and forth on parallel tracks, used to assemble and service a large rocket on its launching pad. Often shortened to "gantry." Also called service tower. This structure is a latticed arrangement of girders, tubing, platforms, cranes, elevators, instruments, wiring, floodlights, cables, and ladders — all used to attend the rocket.

Garbage. Miscellaneous objects in orbit, usually material ejected or broken away from a launch vehicle or satellite.

Geophysics. The physics of the earth and its environment, i.e., earth, air, and (by extension) space.

Gox. Gaseous oxygen.

Gravitation. The acceleration produced by the mutual attraction of two masses, directed along the line joining their centers of mass, and of magnitude inversely proportional to the square of the distance between the two centers of mass.

Gravity. The force imparted by the earth to a mass on or close to the earth. Since the earth is rotating, the force observed as gravity is the resultant of the force of gravitation and the centrifugal force arising from this rotation.

g-suit or G-suit. A suit that exerts pressure on the abdomen and lower parts of the body to prevent or retard the collection of blood below the chest under positive acceleration.

g-tolerance. A tolerance in a person or other animal, or in a piece of equipment, to an acceleration of a particular value.

Guidance. The process of directing the movements of an aeronautical vehicle or space vehicle, with particular reference to the selection of a flight path or trajectory.

Gyro. A device which utilizes the angular momentum of a spinning rotor to sense angular motion of its base about one or two axes at right angles to the spin axis. Also called gyroscope.

Heat shield. Any device that protects something from heat.

Hold. During a countdown: to halt the sequence of events until an impediment has been removed so that the countdown can be resumed, as in "T minus 40 and holding."

Hot test. A propulsion system test conducted by actually firing the propellants.

Human engineering. The art or science of designing, building, or equipping mechanical devices or artificial environments to the anthropometric, physiological, or psychological requirements of the men who will use them.

Hypoxia. Oxygen deficiency in the blood, cells, or tissues of the body in such degree as to cause psychological and physiological disturbances. Hypoxia may result from a scarcity of oxygen in the air being breathed, or from an inability of the body tissues to absorb oxygen under conditions of low ambient pressure. In the latter case, water vapors from body fluids increase in the sacs of the lungs, crowding out the oxygen.

Igniter. Any device used to begin combustion, such as a spark plug in the combustion chamber of a jet engine, or a squib used to ignite fuel in a rocket.

Impact area. The area in which a rocket strikes the earth's surface. Used specifically in reference to the "impact area" of a rocket range.

Impact bag. An inflatable bag attached to a spacecraft or reentry capsule to absorb part of the shock of landing.

Inertial guidance. Guidance by means of acceleration measured and integrated within the craft.

Injection. The process of putting an artificial satellite into orbit. Also the time of such action.

Ionosphere. The part of the earth's outer atmosphere where ions and electrons are present in quantities sufficient to affect the propogation of radio waves.

Launch pad. The load-bearing base or platform from which a rocket is launched. Usually called pad.

Launch ring. The metal ring on the launch pad on which a missile stands before launch.

Launch vehicle. Any device which propels and guides a spacecraft into orbit about the earth or into a trajectory to another celestial body. Often called booster.

Launch window. An interval of time during which a rocket can be launched to accomplish a particular purpose, as "lift-off occurred 5 minutes after the beginning of the 82-minute launch window."

Libration. A real or apparent oscillatory motion, particularly the apparent oscillation of the moon. Because of libration, more than half of the moon's surface is revealed to an observer on the earth, even though the same side of the moon is always toward the earth, because the moon's periods of rotation and revolution are the same.

Lift-off. The action of a rocket vehicle as it separates from its launch pad in a vertical ascent. A lift-off is applicable only to vertical ascent; a takeoff is applicable to ascent at any angle. A lift-off is action performed by a rocket; a launch is action performed upon a rocket or upon a satellite or spaceship carried by a rocket.

Liquid-propellant rocket engine. A rocket engine fueled with a propellant or propellants in liquid form. Also called liquid-propellant rocket.

Longitudinal axis. The fore-and-aft line through the center of gravity of a craft.

Lox. 1. Liquid oxygen. Used attributively as in "lox tank," "lox unit." Also called loxygen. 2. To load the fuel tanks of a rocket vehicle with liquid oxygen. Hence "loxing."

Mach number. (After Ernst Mach, 1838–1916, Austrian scientist.) A number expressing the ratio of the speed of a body or of a point on a body with respect to the surrounding air or other fluid, or the speed of a flow, to the speed of sound in the medium; the speed represented by this number. If the Mach number is less than one, the flow is called subsonic and local disturbances can propagate ahead of the flow. If the Mach number is greater than one, the flow is called supersonic and disturbance cannot propagate ahead of the flow, with the result that shock waves form.

Main stage. 1. In a multistage rocket, the stake that develops the greatest amount of thrust, with or without booster engines. 2. In a single-stage rocket vehicle powered by one or more engines, the period when full thrust (at or about 90 percent) is attained. 3. A sustainer engine, considered as a stage after booster engines have fallen away, as in "the main stage of the Atlas."

Manometer. An instrument for measuring pressure of gases and vapors both above and below atmospheric pressure.

Mass. The measure of the amount of matter in a body, thus its inertia. The weight of a body is the force with which it is attracted by the earth.

Mate. To fit together two major components of a system.

Meteor. In particular, the light phenomenon which results from the entry into the earth's atmosphere of a solid particle from space: more generally, any physical object or phenomenon associated with such an event.

Meteorite. A meteoroid which has reached the surface of the earth without being completely vaporized.

Meteoroid. A solid object moving in interplanetary space, of a size considerably smaller than an asteroid and considerably larger than an atom or molecule.

Micrometeorite. A very small meteorite or meteoritic particle with a diameter in general less than a millimeter.

Missile. Any object thrown, dropped, fired, launched, or otherwise projected with the purpose of striking a target. Short for "ballistic missile," "guided missile." "Missile" is loosely used as a synonym for "rocket" or "spacecraft" by some careless writers.

Mock-up. A full-sized replica or dummy of something, such as a spacecraft, often made of some substitute material, such as wood, and sometimes incorporating functioning pieces of equipment, such as engines.

Module. 1. A self-contained unit of a launch vehicle or spacecraft which serves as a building block for the overall structure. The module is usually designated by its primary function as "command module," "lunar landing module," etc. 2. A one-package assembly of functionally associated electronic parts; usually a plug-in unit.

Multistage rocket. A vehicle having two or more rocket units, each unit firing after the one in back of it has exhausted its propellant. Normally, each unit, or stage, is jettisoned after completing its firing. Also called a multiple-stage rocket or, infrequently, a step rocket.

Nano. A prefix meaning divided by one billion, as in "nanosecond," one-billionth of a second.

Newton's laws of motion. A set of three fundamental postulates forming the basis of the mechanics of rigid bodies, formulated by Newton in 1687.

The first law is concerned with the principle of inertia and states that if a body in motion is not acted upon by an external force, its momentum remains constant (law of conservation of momentum). The second law asserts that the rate of change of momentum of a body is proportional to the force acting upon the body and is in the direction of the applied force. The third law is the principle of action and reaction, stating that for every force acting upon a body there exists a corresponding force of the same magnitude exerted by the body in the opposite direction.

Nose cone. The cone-shaped leading end of a rocket vehicle, consisting (a) of a chamber or chambers in which a satellite, instruments, animals, plants, or auxiliary equipment may be carried, and (b) of an outer surface built to withstand high temperatures generated by aerodynamic heating.

Nozzle. Specifically, the part of a rocket thrust chamber assembly in which the gases produced in the chamber are accelerated to high velocities.

Orbit. 1. The path of a body or particle under the influence of a gravitational or other force. For instance, the orbit of a celestial body in its path relative to another body around which it revolves. 2. To go around the earth or other body in an orbit.

Orbital period. The interval between successive passages of a satellite.

Orbital velocity. 1. The average velocity at which an earth satellite or other orbiting body travels around its primary. 2. The velocity of such a body at any given point in its orbit, as in "its orbital velocity at the apogee is less than at the perigee."

Payload. 1. Originally, the revenue-producing portion of an aircraft's load, *e.g.,* passengers, cargo, mail, etc. 2. By extension, that which an aircraft, rocket, or the like carries over and above what is necessary for the operation of the vehicle during its flight.

Perigee. That orbital point nearest the earth when the earth is the center of attraction. That orbital point farthest from the earth is called apogee. Perigee and apogee are used by many writers in referring to orbits of satellites, especially artificial satellites, around any planet or satellite, thus avoiding coinage of new terms for each planet and moon.

Physiological acceleration. The acceleration experienced by a human or an animal test subject in an accelerating vehicle.

Pitchover. The programmed turn from the vertical that a rocket under power takes as it describes an arc and points in a direction other than vertical. Also known as pitch. *See also* Yaw; Roll.

Planet. A celestial body of the solar system, revolving around the sun in a nearly circular orbit, or a similar body revolving around a star.

Posigrade rocket. An auxiliary rocket fires in the direction in which the vehicle is pointed, used for example in separating two stages of a vehicle.

Pressure suit. A garment designed to provide the human body with an environment above ambient pressure so that respiratory and circulatory functions may continue normally, or nearly so, under low-pressure conditions, such as occur at high altitudes or in space without benefit of a pressurized cabin.

Pressurized. Containing air, or other gas, at a pressure that is higher than the pressure outside the container.

Prestage. A step in the action of igniting a large liquid rocket taken prior to the ignition of the full flow, and consisting of igniting a partial flow of propellants into the thrust chamber.

Primary body. The spatial body about which a satellite or other body orbits, or from which it is escaping, or toward which it is falling. The primary body of the moon is the earth; the primary body of the earth is the sun.

Probe, or space probe. Any device inserted in an environment for the purpose of obtaining information about the environment; specifically, an instrumented vehicle moving through the upper atmosphere or space, or landing upon another celestial body in order to obtain information about the specific environment.

Propellant: *See* Rocket propellant.

Radiation. *See* Electromagnetic radiation.

Radiation pressure. Pressure exerted upon a body by electromagnetic radiation incident upon body.

Radiation shield. 1. A device used on certain types of instruments to prevent unwanted radiation from biasing the measurement of a quantity. 2. A device used to protect bodies from the harmful effects of nuclear radiation, cosmic radiation, or the like.

Radio astronomy. The study of celestial objects through observation of radio frequency waves emitted or reflected by these objects.

Reaction engine. An engine that develops thrust by its reaction to ejection of a substance from it; specifically, such an engine that ejects a jet or stream of gases created by the burning of fuel within the engine. A reaction engine operates in accordance with Newton's third law of motion, *i.e.,* to every action (force) there is an equal and opposite reaction. Both rocket engines and jet engines are reaction engines.

Readout. The action of a radio transmitter transmitting data either instantaneously with the acquisition of the data or by play of a magnetic tape upon which the data have been recorded.

Readout station. A recording or receiving radio station at which data are received from a transmitter in a probe, satellite, or other spacecraft.

Recovery. The procedure or action that obtains when the whole of a satellite, or a section, instrumentation package, or other part of a rocket vehicle is recovered after a launch; the result of this procedure.

Recycle. In a countdown: To stop the count and to return to an earlier point in the countdown, as in "we have recycled, now at T minus 80 and counting." See Hold.

Reentry. The event occurring when a spacecraft or other object comes back into the sensible atmosphere after being rocketed to altitudes above the sensible atmosphere; the action involved in this event.

Reentry vehicle. A space vehicle designed to return with its payload to earth through the sensible atmosphere.

Reentry window. The area at the limits of the earth's atmosphere through which a spacecraft in a given trajectory can pass to accomplish a successful reentry.

Regenerative cooling. The cooling of a part of an engine by the propellant being delivered to the combustion chamber; specifically, the cooling of a rocket-engine combustion chamber or nozzle by circulating the fuel or oxidizer, or both, around the part to be cooled.

Rendezvous. The event of two or more objects meeting at a preconceived time and place. A rendezvous would be involved, for example, in servicing or resupplying a space station.

Retrorocket. (From "retroacting.") A rocket fitted on or in a spacecraft, satellite, or the like to produce thrust opposed to forward motion.

Revolution. Motion of a celestial body in its orbit; circular motion about an axis usually external to the body. In some contexts the terms "revolution" and "rotation" are used interchangeably; but with reference to the motions of a celestial body, "revolution" refers to the motion in an orbit or about an axis external to the body, while "rotation" refers to motion about an axis within the body. Thus, the earth revolves about the sun annually and rotates about its axis daily.

Rocket. 1. A projectile, pyrotechnic device, or flying vehicle propelled by a rocket engine. 2. A rocket engine.

Rocket engine. A reaction engine that contains within itself, or carries along with itself, all the substances necessary for its operation or for the consumption or combustion of its fuel, not re-

quiring intake of any outside substance and hence capable of operation in outer space. Also called rocket motor.

Rocket propellant. Any agent used for consumption or combustion in a rocket and from which the rocket derives its thrust, such as a fuel, oxidizer, additive, catalyst, or any compound or mixture of these. "Rocket propellant" is often shortened to "propellant."

Roll. The rotational or oscillatory movement of an aircraft or similar body which takes place about a longitudinal axis through the body — called roll for any amount of such rotation. See also Pitch.

Rotation. Turning of a body about an axis within the body, as the daily rotation of the earth. See Revolution.

Satellite. 1. An attendant body that revolves about another body, the primary; especially in the solar system, a secondary body, or moon, that revolves about a planet. 2. A man-made object that revolves about a spatial body, such as Explorer I orbiting about the earth.

Scrub. To cancel a scheduled rocket firing, either before or during countdown.

Selenographic. 1. Of or pertaining to the physical geography of the moon. 2. Specifically, referring to positions on the moon measured in latitude from the moon's equator and in longitude from a reference meridian.

Sensor. The component of an instrument that converts an input signal into a quantity which is measured by another part of the instrument. Also called sensing element.

Shot. An act or instance of firing a rocket, especially from the earth's surface, as "the shot carried the rocket 200 miles."

Sidereal. Of or pertaining to the stars.

Solar radiation. The total electromagnetic radiation emitted by the sun.

Solid propellant. Specifically, a rocket propellant in solid form, usually containing both fuel and oxidizer combined or mixed and formed into a monolithic (not powdered or granulated) grain. See Rocket propellant.

Solid-propellant rocket engine. A rocket engine using a solid propellant. Such engines consist essentially of a combustion chamber containing the propellant, and a nozzle for the exhaust jet, although they often contain other components, as grids, liners, etc. See Rocket engine.

Solar wind. A stream of protons constantly moving outward from the sun.

Space. 1. Specifically, the part of the universe lying outside the limits of the earth's atmosphere. 2. More generally, the volume in which all spatial bodies, including the earth, move.

Space-air vehicle. A vehicle that may be operated either within or above the sensible atmosphere.

Spacecraft. Devices, manned and unmanned, which are designed to be placed into an orbit about the earth or into a trajectory to another celestial body.

Space medicine. A branch of aerospace medicine concerned specifically with the health of persons who make, or expect to make, flights into space beyond the sensible atmosphere.

Space probe. See Probe.

Space simulator. A device which simulates some condition or conditions existing in space and used for testing equipment, or in training programs.

Splashdown. The atmospheric reentry and landing of a spacecraft in the ocean. *See also* Recovery.

Stage. A propulsion unit of a rocket, especially one unit of a multistage rocket, including its own fuel and tanks.

Stage-and-a-half. A liquid-rocket propulsion unit of which only part falls away from the rocket vehicle during flight, as in the case of booster rockets falling away to leave the sustainer engine to consume remaining fuel.

Stationary orbit. An orbit in which an equatorial satellite revolves about the primary at the same angular rate as the primary rotates on its axis. From the primary, the satellite thus appears to be stationary over a point on the primary.

Sunspot. A relatively dark area on the surface of the sun, consisting of a dark central umbra and a surrounding penumbra that is intermediate in brightness between the umbra and the surrounding photosphere.

Sunspot cycle. A periodic variation in the number and area of sunspots with an average length of 11.1 years, but varying between about 7 and 17 years.

Supersonic. Pertaining to speeds greater than the speed of sound. *See* Ultrasonic.

Sustainer engine. An engine that maintains the velocity of a missile or rocket vehicle, once it has achieved its programmed velocity through use of a booster engine.

Synchronous satellite. An equatorial west-to-east satellite orbiting the earth at an altitude of 22,300 statute miles at which altitude it makes one revolution in 24 hours, synchronous with the earth's rotation.

Tektite. A small glassy body containing no crystals, probably of meteoritic origin, and bearing no antecedent relation to the geological formation in which it occurs.

Telemetry. The science of measuring a quantity or quantities, transmitting the measured value to a distant station, and there interpreting, indicating, or recording the quantities measured.

Terminator. The line separating illuminated and dark portions of a nonluminous body, as the moon.

Terrestrial. Pertaining to the earth.

Thermal. Pertaining to heat or temperature.

Thermodynamic. Pertaining to the flow of heat or to thermodynamics.

Thermodynamics. The study of the relationships between heat and mechanical energy.

Thermonuclear. Pertaining to a nuclear reaction that is triggered by particles of high thermal energy.

Thrust. 1. The pushing force developed by an aircraft engine or a rocket engine. 2. Specifically, in rocketry, the product of propellant mass flow rate and exhaust velocity relative to the vehicle.

Tracking. The process of following the movement of a satellite or rocket by radar, radio, and photographic observations.

Trajectory. In general, the path traced by any body, as a rocket, moving as a result of externally applied forces. Trajectory is loosely used to mean "flight path" or "orbit."

Translunar. Of or pertaining to space outside the moon's orbit about the earth.

T-time. Any specific time, minus or plus, as referenced to "zero," or "launch" time, during a countdown sequence that is intended to result in the firing of a rocket propulsion unit that launches a rocket vehicle or missile.

Ultrasonic. Of or pertaining to frequencies above those that affect the human ear, *i.e.*, more than 20,000 vibrations per second.

Umbilical cord. Any of the servicing electrical or fluid lines between the ground or a tower and an upright rocket missile or vehicle before the launch. Often shortened to "umbilical."

Van Allen belt, Van Allen radiation belt. (For James A. Van Allen, 1915- .) The zone of high-intensity radiation surrounding the earth beginning at altitudes of approximately 500 miles.

Vehicle. Specifically, a structure, machine, or device, such as an aircraft or rocket, designed to carry a burden through air or space; more restrictively, a rocket craft. This word has acquired its specific meaning owing to the need for a term to embrace all flying craft, including aircraft and rockets.

Weight. The force with which an earthbound body is attracted toward the earth.

Weightlessness. A condition in which no acceleration, whether of gravity or other force, can be detected by an observer within the system in question. Any object falling freely in a vacuum is weightless; thus an unaccelerated satellite orbiting the earth is "weightless" although gravity affects its orbit. Weightlessness can be produced within the atmosphere in aircraft flying a parabolic flight path.

Yaw. 1. The lateral rotational or oscillatory movement of an aircraft, rocket, or the like about a transverse axis. 2. The amount of this movement, *i.e.,* the angle of yaw. *See also* Roll.

Zero-g. weightlessness.

INDEX

Agena target vehicle, 35, 36, 64, 66, 68, 72, 74, 76, 77, 78, 80, 81

Aldrin, Edwin E. Jr. ("Buzz"), 36, 80, 81, 83, 87, 111, 116, 117, 118, 119, 120

   addresses Congress, 120

   biography of, 133

Allen, Joseph P. IV, 133

Anders, William A., 86, 96, 97, 98

   biography of, 133

Apollo 1, 21, 46, 85, 88

Apollo 4, 85

Apollo 6, 85

Apollo 7, 85, 90, 91, 92, 93

Apollo 8, 86, 96, 97, 98, 100, 101

Apollo 9, 86, 102, 104

   splashdown, 105

Apollo 10, 86, 87, 106, 107, 108, 109, 110

   splashdown, 110

Apollo 11, 86, 87, 111, 112-120

Apollo 12, 87, 121, 122, 123, 124

   lunar landing area, 123

   splashdown, 126

Apollo 13, 127, 128, 129, 130, 131, 132

   explosion in, 87

   splashdown, 131

Apollo command module, 84, 88

Apollo service module, 84

Apollo space vehicle, 37

Armstrong, Neil A., 35, 64, 67, 87, 111, 117, 119

   biography of, 133-134

   first step on moon, 115

Atlas 6 booster rocket (Project Mercury), 23, 29

Augmented Target Docking Adapter (ATDA), 69

Aurora 7 (Carpenter), 8, 26

Auto pilot, 32

Bassett, Charles A. II, 134

Bean, Alan L., 87, 121, 124, 126

   biography of, 134

Bio-sensors, 15

Borman, Frank, 35, 54, 57, 58, 59, 62, 86, 96, 97, 100, 101

   biography of, 134

Brand, Vance D., 134

Breccia, 126

Cape Canaveral, 8, 12, 20

Carpenter, M. Scott, 8, 9, 26, 27, 33

   biography of, 134-135

Carr, Gerald P., 135

Centrifuge testing, 14

Cernan, Eugene A., 36, 68, 70, 71, 86, 106, 108

   biography of, 135

Chaffee, Roger B., 85, 88

   biography of, 135

Chapman, Philip K., 135

"Charlie Brown" (LCM), 108

"Cherry Picker," 10

Cocoa Beach, Florida, 22

Collins, Michael, 36, 72, 74, 75, 87, 111, 119

   biography of, 135-136

Command service module (CSM), 107, 109. *See also* Lunar command module (LCM)

Complex 19 (Cape Kennedy), 39, 68

Conrad, Charles Jr., 34, 36, 50, 53, 76, 87, 121, 124

   biography of, 136

Cooper, L. Gordon Jr. ("Gordo"), 8, 9, 12, 30, 31, 32, 33, 34, 50, 53

   biography of, 136

Core sample, from moon, 124

Crippen, Robert L., 136

Cunningham, R. Walter, 85, 91, 94

   biography of, 136-137

Descent stage, of lunar module, 119

Docking maneuver, 35, 36, 38, 66, 92, 102

Duke, Charles M. Jr., 137

Early Apollo Scientific Experiments Package (EASEP), 117

Earth rise, 86, 100, 110, 113

Earth, view of

   from Apollo 7, 95

   from Apollo 11, 112, 113

   from Faith 7, 31

   from Gemini 4, 48, 49

   from Gemini 5, 51

   from Gemini 10, 74

   from Gemini 11, 79

   from lunar orbit, 100

Eisele, Donn F., 85, 91, 93, 94, 95

   biography of, 137

Ejection mechanism, 60

Ejection seats, 38

Ellington Air Force Base, Texas, 38

England, Anthony W., 137

Engle, Joe H., 137

Equipment

   for Gemini 4, 45

   for Gemini 7, 55

Equipment
    for Gemini 8, 65
    for Project Mercury, 11
    left on moon, 118
Evans, Ronald E., 137-138
Extravehicular activity (EVA), 36, 46, 78, 80, 103, 105,
    124
    on moon, 87, 117
    See also "Space walk"

Faith 7 (Cooper), 8, 30, 31, 32
Flag on moon, 116
Flash fire on Apollo 1, 21, 46, 85, 88
Food
    for Gemini 7, 55
    for Project Mercury, 15
Footprints on moon, 115
Formation flight (Gemini 11), 77
Fra Mauro region of moon, 127
Freeman, Theodore C., 138
Friendship 7 (Glenn), 7, 8, 22, 24
Frogmen. *See* Pararescuemen
Fuel cells, 38
    breakdown of on Gemini 5, 52
Fullerton, Charles G., 138
Garriott, Owen K., 138
Gemini
    meaning of, 34
    space vehicle, 37, 38
    suit, 45
Gemini 3, 34, 39, 40, 42, 43, 72
Gemini 4, 34, 44, 45, 46, 49
Gemini 5, 34, 50, 52
Gemini 6, 35, 54, 58, 60, 61
Gemini 7, 35, 54, 55, 57, 59, 62, 63
Gemini 8, 35, 64, 66
Gemini 9, 36, 68, 69, 70, 71
    splashdown, 70
Gemini 10, 36, 72, 73, 74
Gemini 11, 36, 76, 77
Gemini 12, 36, 80
    splashdown, 82
Genesis, reading of from space, 86, 101
Gibson, Edward G., 138
Givens, Edward G. Jr., 138-139
Glenn, John H. Jr., 8, 9, 12, 14, 22, 23, 24, 25
    biography of, 139
"Golden slippers," 105
Gordon, Richard F. Jr., 36, 76, 77, 78, 87, 121, 124
    biography of, 139
Grand Bahama Island, 20
Grand Turk Island (West Indies), 43
Grissom, Virgil I. ("Gus"), 8, 9, 12, 20, 21, 33, 34, 38, 40,
    41, 42, 43, 46
    biography of, 139

Grissom, Virgil I. ("Gus")
    death of in Apollo 1, 85, 88
"Gumdrop" (LCM), 103, 104, 105

Haise, Fred W. Jr., 87, 127, 131, 132
    biography of, 139
Henize, Karl G., 139-140
Holmquest, Donald L., 140

Iconorama display, 52
Inertial guidance system, 38
Irwin, James B., 140

Johnson, Lyndon B., 33, 43, 53, 71, 101
Johnsville, Pa., 14

Kennedy, John F., 25, 33
Kennedy Space Center, 93
Kerwin, Joseph P., 140
Kraft, Christopher C. Jr., 56

Laser-beam transmission, 35
Launch Complex 34 (Cape Kennedy), 88, 90
Launch control center, 113
Lenoir, William B., 140
Liberty Bell 7 (Grissom), 20, 21
Limb, 49
Lind, Don L., 140
Loss of signal (LOS), 99
Lousma, Jack R., 140-141
Lovell, James A. Jr., 35, 36, 54, 57, 59, 62, 80, 81, 86,
    87, 96, 97, 127, 131, 132
    biography of, 141
Lunar command module (LCM), 103, 104. *See also*
    "Gumdrop," "Charlie Brown"
Lunar excursion module (LEM or LM), 84, 85, 86, 87,
    103, 105, 106, 107, 114, 122
    as "lifeboat," 87, 129, 130
    See also "Snoopy," "Spider"
Lunar landing, 87
Lunar orbit, 99
Lunar Orbiter 3, 123
Lunar samples, 120, 126

McCandless, Bruce II, 141
McDivitt, James A., 34, 44, 49, 86, 102, 104
    biography of, 142
McDonnell Aircraft Corporation, 38
"Mailbox," device in Apollo 13, 130
Mathews, Charles W., 113
Mattingly, Thomas K. II, 127
    biography of, 141-142
Mercury capsule, 10, 26
    compared to Gemini and Apollo, 37
Mission Control Center, 56, 98

Mission Operations Control Room, 56
Mitchell, Edgar D., 142
Mobile Quarantine Facility, 126
Moon landing. *See* Lunar landing
Moon, photos of, 99, 107, 109
    first step on, 115
Moon walk, simulation, 128
Musgrave, F. Story, 142

National Aeronautics and Space Administration
        (NASA), 9, 52, 132
    Exceptional Service Medal, 43
Nixon, Richard M., 116, 120
North American Air Defense Command (NORAD), 52

Ocean of Storms, 87, 123, 125, 127
On-board propulsion, 38
Original astronauts, 9
Overmyer, Robert F., 142

Pad 19 (Cape Kennedy), 42, 61
Pararescuemen, 29, 32, 52, 62, 67, 75, 83, 126
Parker, Robert A., 142
Philips, Samuel C., 113
Plaque on moon, 116
Pogue, William R., 142-143

Quarantine of astronauts, 120

Redstone booster rocket (Project Mercury), 10, 12
Rendezvous in space, 35, 36, 58, 62, 80, 102, 108, 119
Rendezvous radar, 38
Roosa, Stuart A., 143

Saturn 1B booster rocket, 85, 90, 92
Saturn 5 booster rocket, 85, 86, 97, 103, 122
    first manned flight with, 96
Schirra, Walter M. Jr., 8, 9, 28, 29, 33, 35, 60, 61, 62, 63,
        85, 91, 93, 95
    biography of, 143
Schmitt, Harrison H., 143
Schweickart, Russell L., 86, 102, 104, 105
    biography of, 143-144
Scott, David R., 35, 64, 65, 66, 67, 86, 102, 103, 104
    biography of, 144
Sea of Tranquility, 114
See, Elliot M. Jr., 144
Shepard, Alan B. Jr., 8, 9, 12, 19, 33
    biography of, 144
Sigma 7 (Schirra), 7, 8, 28, 29
Slayton, Donald K. ("Deke"), 9
    biography of, 144
"Snoopy" (LM), 108

Solar eclipse, 36
Solar Wind Composition equipment, 118
Space
    docking maneuver in, 35, 36
    food, 7, 15, 55
    living and working in, 30
    navigating in, 35
    rendezvous in, 35, 36, 58, 62, 68, 80
"Space Twins," 43. *See also* Grissom, Young
Space vehicles, compared, 37
"Space walk," 34, 36, 44, 46, 68, 74, 76. *See also*
        Extravehicular activity
"Spider" (LEM), 103
Stafford, Thomas P., 36, 60, 61, 63, 68, 69, 71, 86, 106,
        108
    biography of, 145
Surveyor 3, 123, 124
Swigert, John L., 87, 127, 130, 131, 132
    biography of, 145

Television from space, 86, 87, 93, 94, 98
    failure of in Apollo 12, 126
Testing
    for Gemini 5, 50
    for Gemini 9, 68
    for Project Mercury, 14
Thermal sample, 105
Thornton, William E., 145
Titan booster rocket (Gemini), 39, 41, 73, 76, 85
Tracking stations, 52
Training, for Project Gemini, 38
Tranquility Base, 116
Triesnecker Crater, 109
Truly, Richard H., 145

U.S.S. *Essex,* 95
U.S.S. *Guadalcanal,* 75, 105
U.S.S. *Guam,* 76
U.S.S. *Hornet,* 120, 126
U.S.S. *Intrepid,* 27, 43
U.S.S. *Iwo Jima,* 87, 131, 132
U.S.S. *Kearsarge,* 29, 32
U.S.S. *Lake Champlain,* 52, 53
U.S.S. *Mason,* 67
U.S.S. *Noa,* 24
U.S.S. *Princeton,* 110
U.S.S. *Randolph,* 25
U.S.S. *Wasp,* 49, 58, 62, 63, 71, 83
U.S.S. *Yorktown,* 101

Von Braun, Wernher, 113

Weightlessness, demonstrated in Apollo 10, 109

Weitz, Paul J., 145-146
White, Edward H., 34, 44, 45, 46, 49
   biography of, 146
   death of in Apollo 1, 85, 88
   "space walk" of, 34, 44, 45, 46
White House reception for astronauts, 33
White Room (Cape Kennedy), 39, 41, 61, 64, 88, 122

Williams, Clifton C. Jr., 146
Worden, Alfred M., 146

Young, John W., 34, 36, 38, 40, 41, 42, 43, 72, 75, 86,
   106, 108
   biography of, 146

SPECIAL SUPPLEMENT
THE APOLLO 14 AND APOLLO 15 MISSIONS

The official emblems of the Apollo 14 and Apollo 15 lunar missions. Each mission emblem is the property of the U.S. government and is authorized for wear by the astronauts only.

Prime crew of the Apollo 14 lunar mission pose before their official emblem at Kennedy Space Center, Florida. Center, mission commander Alan B. Shepard; left, command module pilot Stuart Roosa; and right, lunar module pilot Edgar Mitchell.

Above, astronaut Shepard waves to crowd gathered to watch him and his fellow astronauts leave the Manned Spacecraft Operations Building at the start of their 9-mile trip to Launch Complex 39A.

The mighty Saturn 5 space vehicle lifts off slowly but surely, propelling astronauts Shepard, Roosa, and Mitchell moonward with its 7½ million pounds of thrust. Lift-off was recorded at 4:03 P.M. on January 31, 1971, sending the three astronauts on the first leg of their lunar voyage.

Above, lunar module stands on the moon's surface after the successful 109-hour journey from earth. Landing was pinpointed within yards of the target in the hilly and difficult Fra Mauro region of the moon. "There was not a smooth place anywhere near the site," Shepard remarked. Below, "It's been a long way, but we are here," said Shepard as his feet touched the lunar surface. Shepard, who had worked twelve years for this shot at the moon, thus fulfilled his long-sought goal of walking on the earth's natural satellite. Shot shows Shepard during the first EVA activity, with work checklist worn on his wrist. In background, Mitchell works at deployment site of the Apollo Lunar Surface Experiments Package (ALSEP).

Astronaut Mitchell moves across the lunar surface during EVA. Lunar dust can be seen clinging to the boots and legs of his space suit.

Below, Alan Shepard stands beside a large boulder on his "mountain climb" toward Cone Crater. Terrain was so difficult, the men had to turn back 300 feet short of their objective—the crater rim. Nevertheless, of more than 215 lunar surface tasks, Shepard and Mitchell completed all but nine in a breathless 9 hours and 19 minutes outside the LM.

Astronaut Mitchell pauses during a later EVA excursion to unload one of the Apollo lunar hand tools from the Modularized Equipment Transporter (MET). Although there was trouble with the Abort Guidance System after lift-off from the moon, the crew successfully rendezvoused with command module pilot Stuart Roosa.

The Apollo 14 spacecraft containing the three astronauts parachutes safely into the Pacific Ocean at the completion of the 9-day lunar voyage. Splashdown occurred 780 nautical miles southeast of Samoa.

The Apollo 14 astronauts watch a Navy pararescueman close the hatch of their spacecraft during recovery operations. Below, Mitchell (left, pointing), Roosa (center), and Shepard (right) show off some of the larger lunar rock samples which they brought back from the moon. Occasion was a through-the-glass meeting with newsmen in the Crew Reception Area of the Lunar Receiving Laboratory at the Manned Spacecraft Center in Houston during the mandatory quarantine period.

Prime crew of the Apollo 15 lunar mission pose in space suits beneath their official emblem. From left are David R. Scott, mission commander; Alfred M. Worden, command module pilot; and James B. Irwin, lunar module pilot.

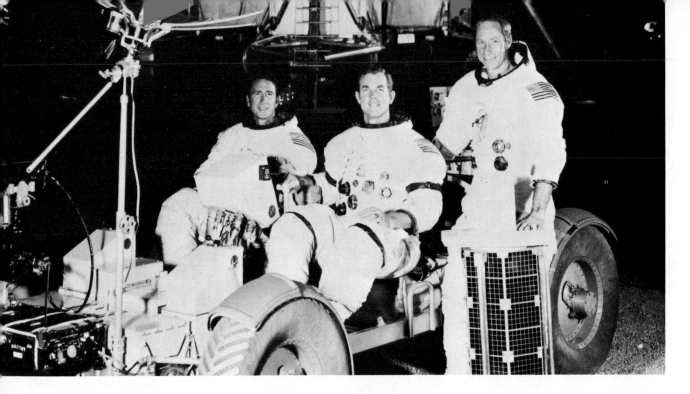

Apollo 15 astronauts display the Lunar Rover. Battery-powered Rover is equipped with a TV camera which is used when the vehicle is parked, and can be controlled from the ground while astronauts explore the moon. Below, astronauts relax during suiting activities prior to launch. Lying in foreground is Scott, then Worden and Irwin. Irwin's bubble helmet is covered to shield the light during his brief catnap. At left is Donald K. ("Deke") Slayton, chief of Flight Crew Operations and himself an early astronaut.

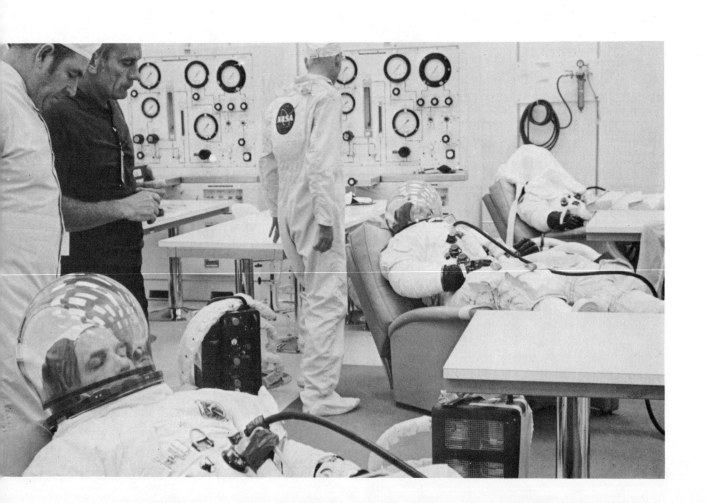

Apollo 15 astronauts lift off successfully aboard an Apollo Saturn 5 space vehicle at 9:34 A.M. on July 26, 1971. The 363-foot-high booster generated 7½ million pounds of thrust as it sent the men on the first leg of their quarter-of-a-million-mile journey to the moon.

The Apollo 15 lunar module touched down at the Hadley-Apennine site at 6:16 P.M., EDT, July 30, and stayed on the lunar surface a total time of 66 hours, 55 minutes. Astronaut Irwin is saluting the flag, with LM in center and Lunar Rover parked at right. Hadley Delta is in the background and St. George's Crater is behind the Rover about 5 kilometers away. Below, Apollo 15 TV picture shows Scott (left) and Irwin gathering rock samples during their second EVA. Transmission was made by color TV camera mounted on the Lunar Rover.

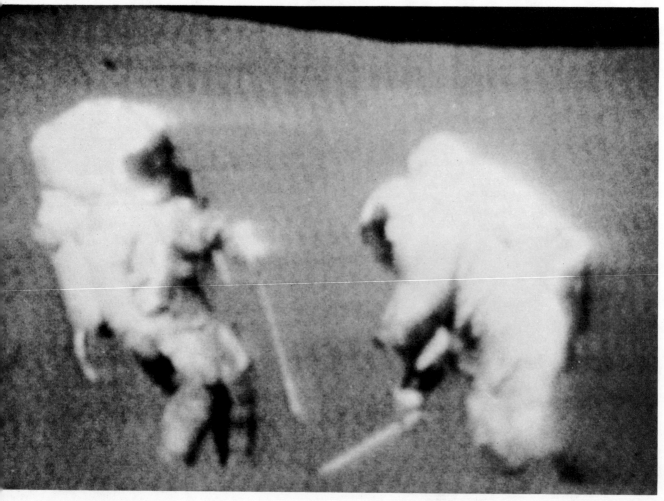

Scott is shown here at the Rover on the edge of Hadley Rille. Irwin, who took photo, was standing on the flank of St. George's Crater.

Close-up of Lunar Rover parked near the lunar module. View is looking northeast, with Mount Hadley in the background.

James Irwin walks away from the Rover during EVA to attend to scientific tasks. Rover is parked near the edge of Hadley Rille. Far wall of the rille appears in the distance at upper left. Below, blurred but dramatic TV shot shows the Apollo 15 lunar module "Falcon" ascent stage making its lift-off from the lunar surface. Transmission was made from the camera mounted on the Lunar Rover, which stayed behind on the moon. Thousands watched the transmission, remotely controlled from earth, as the ascent stage returned from the lunar surface to rejoin the command and service modules orbiting the moon and piloted by astronaut Worden. The return trip to earth went off on schedule.

Drogue chutes ballooning spectacularly, the Apollo 15 spacecraft is recovered successfully by the Navy. Splashdown in the Pacific Ocean was at 4:46 P.M. on August 7, 1971—333 miles north of Hawaii. Below, happy astronauts of Apollo 15 relax as they await helicopter pickup from their life raft during recovery operations at the completion of their highly successful 12-day lunar mission. The astronauts were welcomed aboard the U.S.S. *Okinawa* about 40 minutes after splashdown.

"I think we've found what we came for." So said David Scott (left) on the lunar surface when he first bagged the lunar sample which came to be known as the "genesis rock"—a very early specimen believed to be associated with the origin of the solar system. In photo at right, Scott and Irwin (right) join geologists in getting first looks at some of the Apollo 15 moon rock samples to be opened in the Non-Sterile Nitrogen Processing Line in the Manned Spacecraft Center's Lunar Receiving Laboratory.

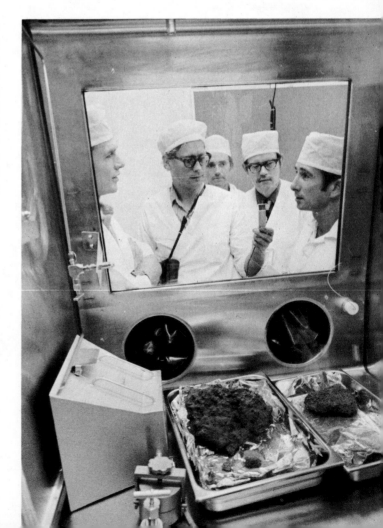